NEW NEIGHBOR

LEROY BARBER

TO THE BROTHERS AND SISTERS
INVOLVED IN MISSION YEAR

EDITOR: Joanna DeWolf
EDITOR: Carmen Williams
ART DIRECTOR: Elizabeth Malpass
CREATIVE DIRECTOR: Jeff Shinabarger

PUBLISHED BY **missionyear**

www.missionyear.org
Copyright © 2008 Mission Year and Leroy Barber

FOR INFORMATION ON BULK ORDERS:
missionyear
PO BOX 17628 Atlanta, GA 30316
Phone: 888-340-YEAR (9327) Fax: 404-880-0028
Email: info@missionyear.org

CHAPTER 1
WHO IS MY NEIGHBOR?

16	NEIGHBOR DEFINED	Leroy Barber
18	THE OLD AND THE NEW	Leroy Barber
22	CRASH	Leroy Barber
26	PIZZA: THE LORD'S SUPPER	Caleb Mechem
28	ASHAMED	Matthew Fowler
30	GETTING GRACE	Jordan Leahy

CHAPTER 2
THIS IS MY NEIGHBOR.

34	TOWEL DRY CONVERSATIONS	Leroy Barber
38	SHE WALKS IN DARKNESS	Leroy Barber
40	IMPROMPTU PARTY	William Owen
42	MRS. BISHOP	Claire Hevel
44	A ROOM FULL OF HOMELESS GUYS	Joe Grove

CHAPTER 3
WHAT'S SO BELOVED ABOUT COMMUNITY?

48	GRAY	Leroy Barber
54	THE MILLERS	Leroy Barber
58	WOULD JESUS DRIVE?	Jeff Delp
64	BROWN-EYED LOVE	Sarah Holliday
66	LESSON LEARNED	Anne Callison

CHAPTER 4
THIS IS MY BELOVED COMMUNITY.

70	ALL OF US	Leroy Barber
72	BARBERSHOP	Leroy Barber
74	CONFESSION	A Letter to Leroy
76	AGONY & ECSTASY	Shawn Casselberry
80	A BITTERSWEET BREAK	Melissa McLamb
82	MISSION YEAR RUINED MY LIFE	Frances Joy Santiago

CHAPTER 5
WHERE IS THE JUSTICE?

86	BLACK ON BLACK	Leroy Barber
88	ENVIRONMENTAL JUSTICE	Leroy Barber
92	WHERE IS THE CHURCH?	Leroy Barber
94	A SINGLE GARMENT OF DESTINY	Nate Martin
96	JESUS IS HERE	Zach Zimbelman
98	SAFER	Lacey Martin

CHAPTER 6
THIS IS MY JUSTICE.

102	HE BELIEVED ME	Leroy Barber
104	MONSTERS	Leroy Barber
110	SEPARATE & UNEQUAL	Leroy Barber
112	ESPERANZA	Jessica O'Brien
116	TEARS OF LOVE	Kristen Fabick
118	TERRIFIED	Holly Waddell

CHAPTER 7
WHERE DO I BEGIN?

122	TWO STONES	Leroy Barber
126	FRIEND WITH MONEY	Leroy Barber
130	HOPE VS. CYNICISM	Leroy Barber
132	REBUILDING	Emily Rhodes
134	ONE MORE THING	Ashley Pharis
136	BROWNIES	Jessica O'Brien

CHAPTER 8
THIS IS MY BEGINNING.

140	O FATHER, WHERE ART THOU?	Leroy Barber
142	PRESIDENT	Leroy Barber
144	A WORD ON HOPE	Leroy Barber
146	A NEW WAY OF LIVING	Carmen Williams
148	THE GIFT OF FRIENDS	Anne Callison
150	PLAYING IT SAFE	Emmy Johnson

CHAPTER 9
WHAT DO I BRING?

154	SONS	Leroy Barber
156	LIVING TOGETHER	Leroy Barber
158	525,600 MINUTES	Leroy Barber
160	FINDING FAMILY	Anonymous
162	"I LOVE YOU"	Josh Phillips
164	TEACH P.E.?!	Heather Bouley

CHAPTER 10
THIS IS WHAT I HAVE.

168	STRENGTH	Leroy Barber
170	A COFFEE SHOP	Leroy Barber
174	NOT LONG ENOUGH	Claire Hevel
176	REMEMBER	Charles Fick

FORWARD

Amidst all the surface discussions about caring for the poor, amidst the flurry of mission trips and weekend service projects and volunteer sign-ups, the affluent (by any standards) commuter church struggles to put into practice the most basic command of the Christian faith – love God and love neighbor. Mission trippers may return from their third world experience with their awareness raised and their hearts stirred, but they are soon assimilated back into their busy schedules and the images that challenged their souls fade from memory. It is the norm for western Christians. And it happens because we live our daily lives in isolation from the poor. Out of sight, out of mind.

New Neighbor is an invitation to become a neighbor right where we live. Here at home. In our own city. The powerful vignettes are the stories of those who have chosen to follow Jesus into neglected places and become neighbors among those many would consider undesirable. Their struggles and tensions have yielded insights vital for the journey of faith. Their examples lead the way toward a new (yet very old) lifestyle consistent with a new command Christ laid on His disciples on their last night together. Doubtless there was good reason why our Lord felt compelled to underscore so emphatically this new command, for to live out this kind of love is an unnatural act. It requires significant self-sacrifice, and leaving one's familiar comfort zone. The "new neighbors" in *New Neighbor* are taking seriously, and quite literally, this business of loving one another – across the barriers of race and class that so badly fracture the Body of Christ and society as a whole. And in the process they are learning that diversity is in fact God's idea, a rich gift through which secrets of the Kingdom are revealed. The biggest surprise of all is discovering that this calling to become a neighbor is at least as much about our own salvation as it is about the redemption of our neighbors.

DR. ROBERT LUPTON

INTRODUCTION

In our rapidly changing culture, our neighbors grow more diverse every day. Socioeconomic, racial, and cultural lines continue to dissolve leaving us a new neighborhood landscape. This is a great time to explore what it means to be a New Neighbor.

A New Neighbor who lets the values of scripture guide in how to love the people around us. A New Neighbor immersed in a multi-ethnic community. A New Neighbor who changes the nature of the public square instead of creating our own separate but Christian way of life. A New Neighbor walking with instead of doing for or handing down. A New Neighbor bringing a much needed voice to our society. A New Neighbor seeking a relationship with the Creator, loving the creatures He created, and stewarding creation. A New Neighbor striving to create a community worth joining.

It is my privilege to offer to you this gallery of images, stories, quotes and journals inspired by neighbors. People caring for the needs of others. Friends choosing to give their time to serve the people that live next door. Individuals setting aside personal agendas for the sake of others. Many of the stories were written by members of Mission Year, a community of people dedicated to loving God and loving people. Together we are discovering the joys and sorrows, challenges and opportunities of living as New Neighbors.

LEROY BARBER

portrait photo: 6offour.com

WHO

IS MY NEIGHBOR?

NEIGHBOR

A man from the crowd asks Jesus a question: "How do I gain eternal life?"

Jesus doesn't give an answer but asks a question: "What does it say in the law?"

The man replies, "To love the Lord with all my heart, soul and strength and love my neighbor as myself."

Jesus replies, "You have answered well."

The man, feeling a little uncomfortable with the situation, then asks one of the biggest questions in scripture: "Who is my neighbor?"

This question echoes through time and makes us just as uncomfortable as it did that man. If we're honest, we too stand in front of Jesus feeling very nervous about the answer to that question. The man asking was a lawyer, an expert in playing with words, elaborating on rules and engaging in arguments. Scripture tells us he asked this question to justify himself. He was playing the lawyer game, because the answer to this question could have some serious social implications. If Jesus says my neighbors are lawyers, then cool. If He says my neighbors are those people I choose to be with, then cool. But if He goes outside my comfort zone, then I have a problem. A lot of us have a problem.

Jesus refuses to play the game. Instead, he tells a story. A certain man goes from Jerusalem to Jericho, and is wounded and beaten along the road and lying half dead. He then describes three responses to this man, obviously in need, lying by the road in plain sight.

A priest comes by and crosses on the other side. He gets as far away from the problem as possible. Perhaps he is protecting himself. Perhaps he is too busy. Perhaps he's seen this before and has grown cold toward it.

DEFINED

A Levite comes by and looks, but keeps on going. Perhaps he thought about helping but felt overwhelmed by the situation. Perhaps this was his first time seeing something like this and he didn't know what to do. Maybe he would share it as an illustration the next time he taught. Maybe he made a mental note to use this as proof to his children of why they should stay away from this road.

A Samaritan comes by and stops. He has compassion, bandages the man's wounds, puts him on his own transportation, gets him a place to stay and offers to pay if it costs any more. The Samaritan showed mercy and Jesus confirms he was indeed a neighbor.

Then Jesus asks the question, "Who was the neighbor to him that fell among the thieves?"

The lawyer answers, "The one who showed mercy."

Jesus stops the justification by changing the question. He answers the question of *who* my neighbor is by telling this man *what* a neighbor is.

A neighbor has compassion, takes time to care for wounds, comforts and then gives on-going support as needed. It doesn't matter the role you play in life. Being a highly respected priest or Levite didn't make those men a neighbor. It doesn't matter what ethnic group you belong to. Being a Jew didn't automatically make any man in the story a neighbor.

Then Jesus gives the command, "Go and do likewise."

Stop worrying about who your neighbor is. Be a neighbor.

THE OLD &

My neighborhood is located in Southeast Atlanta. As I have worked to become a neighbor in this city, I've been confronted time and again with the grip that racism holds on the people here. As we have struggled over the years to overcome this issue, we have learned that part of the solution includes looking at and learning about our past.

By definition, something new requires there to be something old. A new thing becomes all that much more exciting because of our worn out experience with the old. Before we live in the new, we live with the old. For me to become a new neighbor, I need to have a good understanding of what our past neighbors looked like. When we know where we have come from, we get a clearer picture of where to go from here.

The unfortunate history of the United States is that it was heavily founded on slavery. For 250 years, African people were brought to this country on slave ships, bought and sold as goods to work fields in the south. These incredibly evil practices created wealth for their "owners." Finally, the neighbors of the north, many of them followers of Jesus, stood in solidarity with Abraham Lincoln as he gave "The Emancipation Proclamation" in 1862. Slavery ended in 1865.

Eleven years after this victory the Jim Crow laws emerged, legally separating blacks and whites. These were state and local laws enacted primarily but not exclusively in the Southern and border states of the United States between 1876 and 1965. They mandated *de jure* segregation in all public facilities, with a supposedly "separate but equal" status for black Americans and members of other non-white racial groups. In reality, this led to treatment and accommodations that were usually inferior to those provided for white Americans, systematizing a number of economic, educational and social disadvantages. The neighborhood was still divided.

THE NEW

Jim Crow did not end until the Civil Rights movement of the 1960's. The effect was that for nearly 100 years we learned how not to be neighbors. Laws governed eating together at restaurants, living in the same communities and using the same water fountains. These laws dictated where you read library books and even forbade children of different races from playing together.

Jim Crow still showed its ugly face even after the laws were officially gone. Banks redlined black neighborhoods, not giving loans to homes within the boundaries. Realtors played on the fears of white families. They bought homes from whites for less and sold for more to black families looking to own homes for the first time. The country wound up in the 1970's with city neighborhoods and suburban neighborhoods that were separated largely by race and economics.

The horizon has changed today. We see a new trend in cities throughout the United States called gentrification. Gentrification is a dirty word for a lot of people and a cool word for others. For some, it represents white people taking over and displacing blacks. For others, it represents revitalization. It is a tool of injustice for some and a light of hope for others.

The simple definition of gentrification is a change in an urban district or neighborhood brought by an influx of a higher income level than the existing residents. Gentrification can result from urban renewal, which invests in physically deteriorating locales. It brings with it improved access to lending capital for low-income mortgage seekers as their property values increase, increased rates of lending to minority and first-time home purchasers to invest in the appreciating area and improved physical conditions for those renters able to afford the rising rents. Gentrification has been linked to reductions in local property crime rates, increased property prices, increased revenue to local governments from property taxes, increased tolerance of sexual minorities and certain kinds of community activism.

Here's how it played out in my neighborhood.

The government-housing complex near my house was demolished and replaced with new units. My neighbors that rented their homes began to move away because their houses were sold. There were less children playing on the street and the people I used to talk with were gone. The store on the corner closed because someone purchased the building and did not renew their lease. Within a year, the people who would walk by my house everyday were gone, some who had rented for 10, 15 or even 20 years. For the first time, some neighbors complained about my Wednesday and Sunday house church gatherings as well as the basketball hoop sitting out in my driveway.

We have a new YMCA in my neighborhood where my children can go to swim and I go to exercise. The men hanging around near the liquor store are gone because it is now closed. A new gas station and store stand on the corner. The neighborhood now has a Publix supermarket and a bank. A small restaurant and a community center are within walking distance. We now have soccer leagues, swimming pools and golf.

Gentrification is a mixed bag for me. It took away familiar people yet gave me very positive results. It displaced the liquor store as well as my friends. The YMCA replaced my backyard hoop, and I began to see more development than drug deals. The opportunity before me is to pull the good from both sides and create community. My friend, Bob Lupton, calls it Gentrification with Justice.

I call it New Neighbors.

CRASH

The three time Academy Award winning movie *Crash* vividly portrays the collisions of characters from various ethnic and economic backgrounds living in Los Angeles. The resulting racially charged situations, while intense and powerful, solidify many stereotypes that exist in our world today. It would be easy to dismiss this as simply good cinematography. In real life, however, these collisions happen every day. When we "crash" into other people, does it always have to lead to pain? Or can these collisions break stereotypes and build something new?

At twelve years old, I could think of many other places I'd rather be than church on a Friday night. A mother who loved me didn't give me a choice. Pastor Greg Johnson in his suit and tie stood up to teach.

Crash.

Pastor Johnson made the Bible come alive every Friday night through my junior high and high school years. He started with the Bible and used movie and sports analogies that helped it make sense to a teenager. He introduced me to the Kingdom of God and called me to live a radical life. This collision changed my life.

25 years later, I am committed to living in and building the Kingdom of God, leading an organization that intentionally causes collisions.

Amy is comfortable in her white suburban family, attending her white suburban church. A speaker introduces her to Mission Year.

Crash.

With a desire to live out her faith in a radical way, Amy applies for the program and is assigned to Philadelphia, Pennsylvania. She begins

her assignment with Pastor Greg Johnson at Greater Saint Matthew Church.

Crash.

Pastor Johnson's gift of drawing people into responding to Jesus' message about the Kingdom and Amy's passion to serve and be an agent of change come together and lead to some amazing moments. This collision forms a relationship defying stereotypes, breaking down walls of separation and building the Kingdom of God.

In the years following Amy's year of service, Pastor Johnson and Amy's pastor in Seattle have exchanged pulpits, each preaching at the other's church. The youth groups from each church planned and served on a mission trip together to a Native American reservation. The collisions continue.

Every day in our world, an infinite variety of collisions occur. Each person has a choice: focus on the pain and nurse our own wounds or break down a wall and build something new.

PIZZA:

WE SAT
DOWN WITH
THESE FIVE
GUYS AND
ATE PIZZA.

THE LORD'S SUPPER

A couple weeks ago, one of my housemates and I decided to get some pizza and share it with some guys who we've seen sleeping out around City Hall. To be honest, I only went because Jason invited me along; I wasn't particularly excited. I just did it because I didn't have much else to do.

In fact, I was a bit afraid. I'd tried before to meet these fellows and they were pretty uninterested in me.

But we went and we sat down with these five guys and ate pizza. One of them told us a lot of stories about peoples' kindness and God's provisions and they told us a few jokes. After about 15 minutes, I stood up, told them how happy I was to meet them and started to leave. As I walked away one of them said, "Thanks for breaking bread with us!"

His words have stuck with me. All those Sundays that I ate a wafer and drank a sip of grape juice came rushing into my head. What are we doing when we partake in that tradition? I've come to the conclusion that what we're doing is symbolically committing ourselves to one another. Not just to the people we're sharing a pew with or to our congregation or denomination or to the structured American Church. We're committing ourselves to Jesus and to anyone and everyone who remembers Him.

And I think the true beauty must come when we step outside of the symbol. Instead of merely taking part in a two-century-old tradition, let's also share food and talk about our experiences of God with the people that society tells us we should be staying clear of. Business people and homeless veterans, retirees and teenagers, Pacers fans and Pistons fans, Iraqis and Americans: let's all share a table together. After that Saturday afternoon, I'm convinced that that is true Communion.

Let the wafer and the juice be a reminder.

ASHAMED

Tonight our team decided to walk around New Orleans a little bit. While walking, we ran into a man named Ron. Ron smelled like alcohol, was missing most of his teeth and confessed to being homeless. My initial response was to do whatever I could to get this guy to move along so we could continue on with our plans.

But as I began to talk with Ron, I realized how special he was. All Ron wanted to do, once he found out why we were down in New Orleans, was to offer his advice, bless us and pray for us. Ron surprised me; he was probably more knowledgeable about scripture than I am and definitely more caring. I felt, as Ron prayed for us, that this was someone God listens attentively to; that despite being dirty and somewhat smelly, this was someone that God deeply cherishes and I should cherish him too. In that moment I was ashamed of my hard heart and my inability to see Ron for who he truly was: a beloved child of God.

GETTING GRACE

There was a guy who stayed at Breakthrough Men's Center until just about a month ago named Rey. He had been in the program since I started working here in October. He was one of "our" guys. Coming into work was great because you knew Rey was going to be there and you could look forward to hanging out with him.

Rey was one of my boys. He'd moved out of Breakthrough and was struggling a bit. He stopped into the day center from time to time but he was getting by.

This past Monday morning, around 9 o'clock, I got a text message from Rick that informed me Rey had died in his room over the weekend. That was it. I don't remember the last time I talked to him, but it was just that. The last time.

Rey certainly had his struggles. He was an alcoholic, a very visible addiction. He fought it until his last day. It helped bring him to Jesus. He found nowhere else to go but to Him. Alcoholism helped him understand love and grace. I am in no way advocating for alcoholism as a means of evangelism, but Jesus goes for the throat. He goes for what will get us. This is what got Rey and he knew God's grace. Rey "got it." He loved Jesus.

I love you, Rey. See you at the gates. Can't wait to hug you.

WHO

THIS

IS MY NEIGHBOR ?

IS MY NEIGHBOR.

TOWEL DRY

I DON'T WANT
YOUR COINS
I WANT
CHANGE

CONVERSATIONS

I went to wash my car at one of those do-it-yourself places where you vacuum and wash for a pretty reasonable price. I had just returned from taking a group of boys whitewater rafting, so the car was a mess.

"Hey Bro, can I wash it for you?" an elderly gentleman asks as I get out of my car. "I am just trying to earn an honest dollar, bro."

"No I can get it, thanks anyway," I reply as I start vacuuming the inside of my car. I finish the process of vacuuming, wiping the inside and washing the exterior and the man appears again. "I bet you don't have a drying towel!" He was correct; I did not have a way to dry the car. He was there to offer his service. Why not?

"Bro. What's your name?"

"Bobby."

"Go ahead Bobby, dry it for me please."

"You seem like a Christian man, are you?" Bobby asks.

"Why do you say that?"

"Well, you talked to me and most people don't. I figure you must be a Christian man."

"Yeah, I am."

Bobby then begins to tell me his life story.

"I'm 62, born and raised in Lagrange, Georgia. I live here. I live in the closet and watch the place for the owner. I am trying to save up some money to get a room somewhere. I had to leave when I was 13 because I beat up a white man for calling me a nigger. I came to Atlanta and I have been living here since. I used to sleep at Grady hospital and got to know some people there. They gave me a job washing dishes. I did that until I was 22. When I was 22, they told me I had to go to school and learn to read. They could not keep me there any longer unless I learned. I left there and got a construction job and worked there for a long time. I have had a hard life, but if I would have stayed in Lagrange they would have killed me. That was in the 50's, you know? I've been shot seven times, in the hospital a few times, living on the streets. My mother, father and sister are all dead. I've had to make it on my own for a long time. Thanks for giving me some work. I don't like begging."

Bobby dried the car, polished the wheels, cleaned off spots that I missed with incredible pride and detail. He did not want me to pay him for sloppy work. He was so happy to be working for the 45 minutes that I was there, and even happier that I listened to his story as he worked.

I am not sure what to think about his life. It will take me some time to process. I do know that Bobby is a child of God and he had a unique story that not many people have taken the time to hear. I am also aware that to Jesus I probably look a lot like Bobby, and He still takes time to listen.

SHE WALKS

I don't know her name, but I see her get into cars of strange men as they pass through the neighborhood.

I don't know her name, but I watch her as she exits the car, head down in shame.

I don't know her name, but I watch her flag down cars when she's really desperate.

I don't know her name, but she walks in the night as I sleep in my bed.

I don't know her name, but she looks really beat up some days in dirty clothing and ripped stockings.

I don't know her name, but she flashes the cars as they come by in hopes of getting someone to stop.

I don't know her name, but she's wearing high heels and a very short skirt.

I don't know her name, but she is in the car with this old, white guy who doesn't live in our neighborhood.

IN DARKNESS

I do know her name. She used to attend our summer camp.

I do know her name. She graduated from high school last year.

I do know her name. She is in middle school.

I do know her name. She has kids in our camp.

I do know her name. She came by for food last week.

I do know her name. She speaks as she walks by our porch during the day.

Prostitution has an unyielding hold on our neighborhood. Women of all ages and colors walk our streets each day. Young girls are recruited in middle school by pimps who offer everyday necessities, like food and clothing, to get these children started. There is so much innocence lost on our streets and there seem to be no answers. This evil that goes unchecked and unimpeded in our streets takes the purity of young women and leaves them victims to the vices of filthy men. There in the dark and in the shadows, life is stripped away. Resolution is hard to find, but we must actively pursue this dark place to bring light. They have names. They are our neighbors. She is my neighbor.

IMPROMPTU PARTY

One night as I was reading, one of my housemates jumped through the door and exclaimed, without explanation, that we needed to decorate the house. So, with a small supply of balloons and some crêpe paper streamers we turned our narrow wood-paneled living room into, well, a narrow wood-paneled living room with some swiftly placed décor. We then welcomed in one of our neighbors, Fernando, who immediately began crying. The decorations were in celebration of his 37th birthday.

After we finished singing the usual Birthday ditty, he said nothing. A couple minutes later, after he blew out the single candle on the convenience store cupcakes, he explained how much it meant to him. He explained that no one had celebrated the anniversary of his birth all day; no one had remembered this year. He said, "I can't believe that people I've only known for half a year threw me a bigger party than my family."

While we were setting up the rather spontaneous pomp that made up the decorations I doubt any of us thought it would have the impact it did on both our beloved neighbor Fernando and on us. After he thanked each of us personally and gave us all hugs and then a group hug, Fernando left saying it was one of the best birthdays he'd ever had. Near the door after he left, we all stood dumbfounded. We had no idea that a few balloons and streamers and cheap cupcakes could make an adult weep to the point of being speechless. I am constantly blown away by the opportunities that God lays in front of us to learn how to love and to be loved.

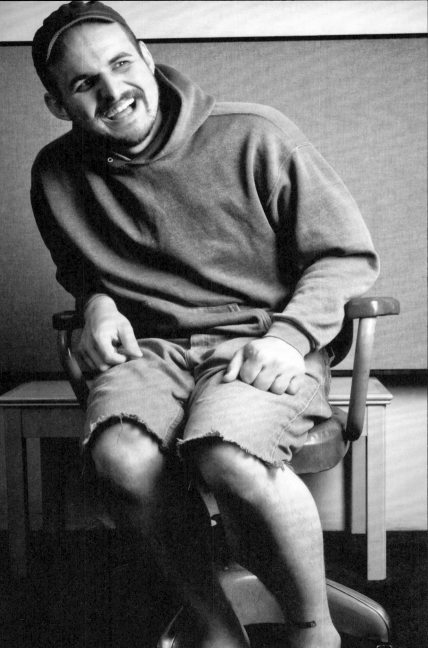

MRS. BISHOP

I met Mrs. Bishop during one of my first walks through my neighborhood. She was sitting outside with her granddaughter. I was with Matt and Seth and we walked by without saying anything. I hesitated, turned my head and said hello. Before I knew it I was talking to Alita (her granddaughter) about her homeschooling and church. I don't remember much from that first day; but, since then, Mrs. Bishop has been a constant in my life.

I don't go to Mrs. Bishop's house expecting to talk with her about everything that happened to me during the week; no, Mrs. Bishop isn't too interested in things like that. Somehow, just by the way she looks at you, you can tell that she is interested in more than just talk. She wants to know how I am feeling about what I am saying and what is going on in my heart. She wants to know what I believe in. She wants to make sure that I am reading the Word and am studying some kind of book or the Bible. She wants to know about me, not the trivial things that happen in life, but me, as an individual. She wants to know what I am passionate about, what I am insecure about, who I love and why I love them. She wants to know where my heart is and if my faith is completely in Jesus.

And let me tell you, Mrs. Bishop does a lot more talking to me than I do talking to her. She wants me to know things. She wants to pour out her knowledge and love into my life. She wants me to know how to have peace and how to be completely content in the love that God has for me. Mrs. Bishop wants me to know that, because of Christ, it is possible for people to love each other no matter what their skin color is. She wants me to know that the only way to get through struggles in life is to have a personal relationship with the Lord. She wants me to know how powerful He is and how sovereign His love is.

Mrs. Bishop is pretty sick; she takes more medication than I can count. Alita is homeschooled so she can take care of her grandmother. I pray for Mrs. Bishop every day. Her health is deteriorating — her physical strength, mind, eyes and body are slowly failing. But I tend to forget about those things. I forget how much physical pain she is in because Mrs. Bishop's heart is bigger than all of that. Her joy, peace, faith and goodness are all that you see — everything else is hidden in the shadow cast by the light that is her love.

A ROOM FULL OF

During devotions today at the Breakthrough Men's Center we talked about Jesus. We talked about how He doesn't care if you're rich or poor. We talked about how He loves everybody the same; the prostitute and the president are equal in His sight. We talked about how there's nothing you can do to make Him stop loving you and there's nothing you can do to earn His love. He just...loves you. We talked about how He was hated by those with wealth and status because wealth and status didn't impress Him. Because He told them that, in heaven, the first will be last and the last will be first.

I spent an hour talking about this with a room full of homeless guys. This is my life.

HOMELESS GUYS

WHAT'S SO BELOVED

ABOUT COMMUNITY?

GRAY

On a normal fall morning in 1995, our day began like most others. A few years before, I had left my job on the custodial staff at a nearby hospital. God had clearly told me to enter full-time ministry by serving the poor and we had been following his direction. There had been many challenges, often financial, but recently the doors had opened for both Donna and I to be on staff at a small Christian school serving our urban neighborhood. Donna, Jess and Josh had left for school already. As was our usual custom, Joel, who was almost two, and I would go later.

I'd dressed Joel, put him on our bed and turned on the television so he could watch Barney while I got ready.

Just as I pulled my shirt down and tucked it into my pants, I sniffed. Smoke. Where was that coming from? I hurried to the top of the stairs and peered down. All I could see was flames! The whole downstairs was on fire!

Snatching Joel up, I ran to the window. When I shoved it open, the draft brought the smoke up the stairs and it poured out the window I was trying to climb through.

The smoke was hot. It hurt to breathe. I held Joel out the window to get fresh air and to keep from getting burned.

Across the street, a contractor was working on a house and he spotted me in the window. He rushed outside and stood right below me. He hollered, "Drop your baby. I'll catch him."

I couldn't think straight. Acrid smoke filled my lungs. The heat from the flames struck my back. I had no idea who this stranger was. Again he yelled, "Let him go, I'll get him."

I had to trust the man.

I loosened my grip and Joel dropped away. The man reached up and grabbed my son, pulling him to his chest. By this time, Joel was crying.

Now I had to find a way to get myself out. I turned back, thinking I might somehow be able to get down the stairs. But by this time, the smoke billowed into the room. Flames crackled. Unbearable heat pressed against me.

I scrambled out of the window and slipped over. For what seemed forever, I clung to the ledge, hoping someone would bring me a ladder. But, there was nothing. No place to put my feet. Nowhere to go.

The smoke surged out the window. It was hot. My hands started to slip. There was nothing to do but let go.

I plunged to the ground, my hip striking the railing to our steps. Somehow I made it across the street and watched my house and a big part of my life go up in flames. The man who saved Joel still held him tightly as he stood next to me. I know he offered me comforting words, but nothing registered. It seemed to take forever for the fire trucks to arrive.

The next thing I remember was a co-worker from the school running toward me. Seth Cohen, a white man with dark hair, about five foot ten and built like a football player, grabbed me and gave me a bear hug. Donna was right behind him, along with many of the school staff. Everyone gathered around calling out, "Are you okay?" "What happened?" "Thank God, you and Joel are okay."

An ambulance arrived and in minutes, I was lying down with an oxygen mask over my face. Donna, with Joel in her arms, rode along with us. We were taken to the emergency room. Everyone bustled around, making sure I was okay. Kind words flowed over me, but I didn't really hear them. All I could think about was that our home was gone. We had nothing but the clothes on our backs. We didn't have insurance or any savings. I had a wife and three children to care for. What a fool I was. What was I going to do?

This was what God gave me for listening to him and going into ministry? I cried. I didn't want anything more to do with God.

As I lay in the hospital, the very one I'd left for this ministry I was involved in, I began praying, "Why have you abandoned me? Why are you making things so hard?" But I didn't receive an answer.

My mom, my pastor and other Christian friends came to see me. All of these people surrounded my bed and began praying. When they began, I felt nothing but cynicism and doubt.

As their prayers continued, I began to feel the power of the Lord surging through me. God whispered to my spirit that I would see Him and know He cared.

Because my hip was extremely sore from hitting the railing when I jumped from the window, I was unable to work. During those days, God showed Himself to me and proved His caring spirit.

It began with our neighbors, who took up a collection to help us restart our lives. Someone called the Red Cross. They brought gift certificates so we could buy clothing. Then something happened that truly surprised and blessed me.

In the weeks just previous to the fire I had shared about our ministry both with my home church, Mt. Zion Baptist, and another church, Wayne Presbyterian. These two churches differed on certain points of theology. Their practices of worship, baptism and church life looked very different every Sunday. Most of the Presbyterians were white, most of the Baptists black. The Presbyterians supported Republicans and the Baptists supported the Democrats. Mt. Zion was located in a struggling community in Southwest Philly. Wayne Presbyterian was out in the suburbs.

What these churches lacked in commonality of belief, method, politics or location faded away that day compared to what they had in common: their love of God and for my family and our work. On Sunday, each church took a special offering and presented us with enough money to rebuild our home. They poured out their compassion on us. They gave out of love and caring. God worked in an amazing way.

This is what I have come to call the shade of gray. Calling something gray is normally thought of as a bad thing — non-commitment and neutrality. I see gray as a place of commonality, a place of community and appreciation. A place of hope. It is where two opposites come together, overlap and find something new and beautiful never before seen.

God came through to me that Sunday in a way that changed my life. Up to that time I'd looked upon the two very different churches as separate and often full of animosity toward each other. On this wonderful day, hope had been returned to me. I saw gray.

We were able to rebuild our home and about 18 months later we moved back in. We invited a group of people from each church, as well as our neighbors, to celebrate our return. And one board that was burned in the fire we left unpainted as a reminder that God not only rebuilds and restores, He also uses even tragedy to create beautiful shades of gray.

THE MILLERS

He is a 75 year old gentleman who lives next door to me and has lived in my neighborhood all of his life. Mr. Miller and his wife keep their property immaculate. They sweep up around it daily, paint their house once a year and keep a well-manicured lawn. The Millers are special people. They have been married for nearly 60 years, and sit on their porch together talking most mornings as I pass by their house. They watch out for our house when we are away and always offer an encouraging word.

Mr. Miller and I have had many conversations about the plight of our neighborhood. He knows it's not in the best shape, but he ends every conversation by saying, "It will all work out in the end." I am a bit more cynical about these things, but Mr. Miller's life keeps speaking in a major way and penetrates my cynicism most of the time. The Millers embody what it means to live good lives in the midst of challenge. They have been sweeping the same pavement, painting the same house and manicuring the same lawn for over 50 years. The Millers are the picture of commitment and dedication.

Dr. King, in describing the beloved community, declares that the universe is on the side of justice and that, eventually, good will prevail over evil. What Dr. King so eloquently wrote and preached is lived out next door to me everyday. This couple may never be famous or see their musings in print, yet they believe that it will all work out in the end. A couple that has lived through racism and Jim Crow in the south still believes.

"I believe Lord, help my unbelief," said the tearful father in Mark 9. Jesus had just declared that with him all things are possible. The man's son was possessed by a demon and had been for a long time. This father wanted to believe Jesus, but the history of his son's behavior loomed large. Life in the city can sometimes be that way. You see

overwhelming problems and a history of hurt and failure in so many lives. It's hard to believe, even though you desperately want to, with so much injustice in front of you.

This is where the Millers' undying commitment helps. People who do the daily things with hope. People who don't give up, but keep doing the right things day after day. People who encourage others by sharing their belief in justice. It is people like the Millers that help us to continue believing.

I believe Lord, help my unbelief.

WOULD JESUS

This morning's journey downtown on the bus started relatively normally for me, waiting for a bus that was ten minutes late. As the bus moved along its route to downtown, it continued to fill up until it was standing room only. The bus was full of people going to work, school or running errands. I was enthralled with a book when I noticed a person in a wheelchair getting onto the bus. Because the bus was packed full, a dozen people had to leave their seats and their standing positions to make room for the person in the wheelchair. Not only that, the thirty other people on the bus had to wait five minutes as the bus driver assisted the person as she got strapped into place.

What amazed me about this process was not that people actually got up or that the bus even had a place for a wheelchair or that the MARTA bus driver was helpful; I was amazed at everyone's reaction on the bus. People got up and moved without saying a word or, if they did say a word, it was to the person in the wheelchair because they knew her. No one on the bus was audibly upset at the bus taking an extra 5 minutes to get downtown because of the person in the wheelchair. It was at that moment that I realized that the bus was a community. We were all part of a community. Our common goal was to get downtown, but we couldn't do it by ourselves; we could only do it together. There was nothing any one person could do, maybe save the bus driver, to get downtown faster. We were all in it together and it benefited all of us to work together so that we could all get downtown faster.

Now, contrast this with a similar example on the highway. Instead of a person with a disability, imagine a car with a disability. A car is disabled on the side of I-75/85 on its way to downtown during the morning commute. In good Atlanta fashion, even though it is pulled off to the side of the road, it slows traffic down. Instead of all of the traffic stopping to wait for the disabled car to get the help it needs

and move on, two or three cars can inch by at a time. Gradually, cars try to move over to the lanes that are allowing traffic through because they, as an individual, can get by and get to where they want to go. The person with the car that is disabled is left until either someone chooses to care or professional help is summoned to their aide.

The two instances provide a stark contrast in how we relate to one another as a society. On the bus, everyone had the same fate and each individual's fate could not be altered by their own actions, no matter how hard they tried (unless they wanted to walk the two miles to downtown). On the highway, each passing car could change their own fate by getting into the correct lane and waiting their turn to get by. What ensued on the bus was a community that allowed space and time for anybody and everybody to get to where they wanted to go equally. What ensues on the highway is an each man for himself, firsts be first mindset in which only those with the means can get by; the disabled driver doesn't get by.

A popular question these days in light of rising gas prices and talk of global warming is, "What Would Jesus Drive?" What if we dropped the "what" and just asked, "Would Jesus Drive?" Taking public transportation often reminds me of the missed opportunities to build relationships when we are sitting behind the wheel of a car. I find myself part of another community when I ride the bus. I think I'll do it more often.

EPHESIANS 2:14-22 (THE MESSAGE)

The Messiah has made things up between us so that we're now together on this, both non-Jewish outsiders and Jewish insiders. He tore down the wall we used to keep each other at a distance. He repealed the law code that had become so clogged with fine print and footnotes that it hindered more than it helped. Then he started over. Instead of continuing with two groups of people separated by centuries of animosity and suspicion, he created a new kind of human being, a fresh start for everybody.

Christ brought us together through his death on the cross. The Cross got us to embrace, and that was the end of the hostility. Christ came and preached peace to you outsiders and peace to us insiders. He treated us as equals, and so made us equals. Through him we both share the same Spirit and have equal access to the Father.

That's plain enough, isn't it? You're no longer wandering exiles. This kingdom of faith is now your home country. You're no longer strangers or outsiders. You belong here, with as much right to the name Christian as anyone. God is building a home. He's using us all — irrespective of how we got here — in what he is building. He used the apostles and prophets for the foundation. Now he's using you, fitting you in brick by brick, stone by stone, with Christ Jesus as the cornerstone that holds all the parts together. We see it taking shape day after day — a holy temple built by God, all of us built into it, a temple in which God is quite at home.

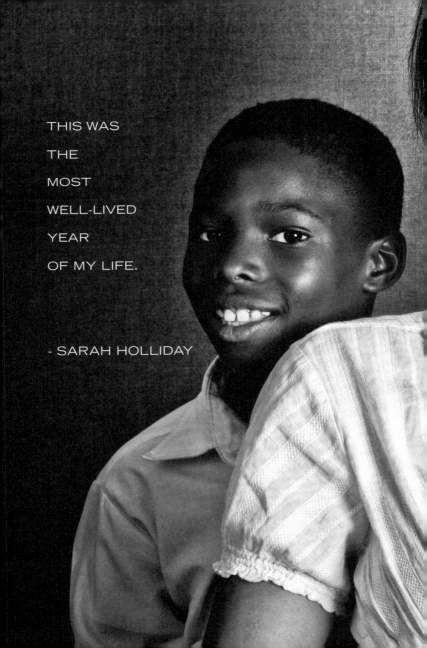

THIS WAS
THE
MOST
WELL-LIVED
YEAR
OF MY LIFE.

- SARAH HOLLIDAY

BROWN-EYED LOVE

I saw Jesus so often in the beautiful faces of all the kids in our neighborhood and at church.

He smiled out at me through big, brown eyes filled with excitement and unrepressed love.

In the form of old men, He gave a friendly word and small talk to me while I sat on, or waited for, a bus and made me feel like a part of the neighborhood.

He was the neighborhood family who always smiled and waved joyously when they saw any of my teammates or me walking by.

He was "Granny" who gave the best hugs on Sundays.

He was the choir at Bethel that always took my breath away with their angelic chords.

He was in the tears of my roommate when she saw some bad things in the neighborhood and her heart cried out for justice.

He was the incredible faith of Mrs. Benson, who lost her husband recently but is not about to let go of her Jesus.

So many memories. So many places I met a whole new Jesus Christ. So many things I still have to process and try to understand. Now, as I stand at the end of this year of service ministry, the one resounding thought I have to sum it all up is: this was the most well-lived year of my life, so far.

LESSON

I am thankful for Miss Smithson who lives just down the street and brightens up my walk from the bus stop. Miss Smithson is an elderly woman of ineffable charm and a love for gardening. She has a gorgeous front yard full of interesting flowers and vegetables. And if you catch her working out in her gardens she loves to stop and chat. She calls us the missionary ladies and she shares recipes, tips for neighborhood safety and her organic produce with us. *Miss Smithson is teaching me about neighborliness...*

I am thankful for Brother Thomas. Thomas is the janitor at our church and we have had the opportunity to spend a good bit of time with him this month. He came over one night for dinner and cards. We had such a wonderful time laughing and joking with him. Thomas is as cheerful a spirit as I can imagine. His smile is contagious. *Brother Thomas is teaching me much about joy...*

I am thankful for the many other neighbors we have met. I am thankful for those who knock on our door or come to our porch in need of a place to sit. I am thankful for those who show up in need of a sandwich or a bus token or something to protect them from the rain. Even when I am tired and drained, I give thanks for their presence. *They are teaching me about the true meaning of care...*

I am thankful for Miss Shirley who lives on the corner and just recently lost her job as a cook. Though she's sure she could get a job back in her hometown of Chicago, she wants to stay in Atlanta to be close with the several grandchildren she has here. We took Miss Shirley to the public library the other day to help her learn to use the computer to look for work. She confessed to us that her true passion is writing. She loves to write scary stories and someday hopes to publish the novel she is working on. *Miss Shirley is teaching me about what it is to dream...*

LEARNED

WHAT'S SO BELOVED

THIS IS MY BELOVED

ABOUT COMMUNITY?
COMMUNITY.

ALL OF US

Aaron was nine years old when Amy and Duffy first brought him to play soccer for a team they help put together. Amy and Duffy were our first married couple to do Mission Year. They connected with this kid who was a bit shy, but athletic. He didn't say much but did a pretty good job on the soccer field. Although he would routinely lose to other teams, he would often manage to find a way to make us laugh and forget the competition with his great smile and laid back demeanor.

Over the next few years, Aaron would get to know a number of Mission Year team members in his neighborhood and attend our church. Aaron played basketball, baseball and soccer coached by team members year after year. Andra and Mike, two team members who remained in Atlanta after their year of service, became youth ministers and spent time with Aaron throughout his teenage years.

Aaron attended summer camp over the past eight years as a camper, then as a junior counselor. He was chosen by the staff to begin learning about what it means to lead. Thoughtful, observant adults seized the opportunity to tap into the potential that Aaron has shown over the years.

At 18, Aaron graduated from high school and became the Assistant Director of the camp he attended for years. He became a peer with another team member serving in Atlanta. And the loved, mentored and taught child has now become the loving, mentoring and teaching adult who gives lessons to Mission Year team members who come to serve as he directs them over the summer.

That fall he attended Albany State as a freshman.

Aaron's story is just one of the many God is writing. When we allow God to write our story, many of us have the privilege of walking the journey with one Aaron. And many Aarons can join us.

BARBERSHOP

Ray Oldenburg in his book, *The Great Good Place* explains the idea of places. Your first place is your home. The second place is your work. In many communities the third place is a coffee shop, pub or even a church. But, my third place is the barbershop.

Every two weeks my sons and I head off to get our hair cut at the neighborhood barbershop. It is a ritual practiced religiously by black men. Moms, dads and young men wait patiently for their barber of choice to cut and fade them just right. We come in looking a little rough around the edges and leave looking smooth.

The barbershop is more than just a place to get an errand checked off the list. It is an experience. The shop is full of conversation about every subject you could imagine: politics, marriage, movies, that day's current event. Nothing compares, however, to sports talk. The atmosphere is electric as each man defends his team. Barbers cutting hair with absolute precision while passionately defending their team's loss over the weekend can only be described as an art form.

This is a place that has been a part of my community life for a long time. My sons have grown up going to this shop. Travis has been our barber for 11 years. We frequently converse about raising children. Travis celebrated with me when my daughter started college. He recognizes my wife and regularly inquires about her. Travis also knows exactly how I like my hair to be cut; I just sit in the chair and he works his magic.

I feel connected in the barbershop. It is familiar, consistent and respected. A place I go that links me to other black men, who may be completely different than I am. The barbershop is an important part of a community that is often overlooked. It is a place where black men relate, converse and relax together. A couple hours away from the world's problems relating to brothers on common ground, the shop is an old neighbor we can't afford to lose.

CONFESSION:

I'm white, but lived in inner-city Atlanta for a couple years, trying to make a difference (both in other people's lives and my own). I am still sifting through the pieces of my life during that time, finding the destruction and the jewels left behind by living out of my element.

One of the things I've noticed is that my racism is still alive, even after a few years of concerted efforts to destroy it. I see it in the little things, but it is those little things that hint at a deeper truth. It is a truth America has been steadfastly resisting for over 450 years. We, as whites, are a deeply racist lot. Many of my friends and family will reject that statement, but consider this: Do you know any chronic disease that has festered for 400 years that can be healed quickly, painlessly and without any special attention? I believe the wound of racism and slavery has closed over, but it has not truly healed. The evidence of this is overwhelming: politicians' and media personalities' continued oblivious and ignorant comments, marked differences in pay based on skin color, the commonly held belief that black history is one of ignorance and petty tribalism. All point not to the inequality of races, but to the inability of whites to look beyond skin color and the refusal of whites to look back at history farther than 30 years to find the source of "black angst."

I have seen it in my own life many, many times. I will give only one example, because it alone serves to condemn me. While in Atlanta, I worked under the city-directorship of a wise, Godly black man. I respected him, but I did not respect him with the level of respect he deserved and earned. With any other race in authority over me, I have always submitted fully. With him, I resisted that tendency to surrender utterly. It was not fear, but that was the problem. With all other authority figures, I had a healthy dose of respect/fear. With my city director, I did not have that same level of respect/fear. I saw him as intelligent, but I did not see him as my head.

A LETTER TO LEROY

Years later, that same attitude caused me to realize how racist I was. I called him up to talk to him and heard that he was no longer a city director. Immediately I assumed that meant he had left the organization. It never crossed my mind that he could have been promoted to President of Mission Year. I quickly rearranged my thinking when I realized he was now the leader of a national organization. I saw clearly that he had not been promoted because of silly reasons, but strictly because of his vision, heart and love of other people. He was, quite literally, the right person for the job, but that first faulty assumption told me all I needed to know about me. It was the death knell ring in my soul. I guess, in some way, this letter is a letter of apology to him.

It is a confession aimed at the soul of racism writhing like a parasite inside my heart. It is still there. I have seen it in my conversations with other blacks, and I both loathe it and feel utterly helpless to remove it. My city director taught me that the only known cure for racism is active, honest friendships. I think he's right. I hope we can engage in those friendships as a nation, or at least in dialogue from the heart. In the end, we need to see each others' hearts.

AGONY

During a recent training with Mary Nelson from Bethel New Life, Inc., she told us that ministry in the city is all about the agony and the ecstasy. We all knew what she meant.

One minute you are celebrating a triumphant moment and the next minute you are mourning a tragedy. We see men and women coming off the streets finding freedom in Christ and others that return to the streets bound to their old addictions. We see teens growing stronger in their faith and becoming leaders in the community and, at the same time, see other teens disengage from school and get involved in gangs. (We have had twenty-three student homicides this year alone.) We see neighbors organizing to resist the negative forces that threaten the well-being of their neighborhoods and others that fatalistically give up all hope for change. It's agony and it's ecstasy. It's smiles and cries.

Our ministry is sharing in the laughter and the tears of our neighbors. In this way, we live the cross and the resurrection daily. Our ministry is not an evangelistic technique or tool; it is sharing all of our lives with people. This means that the agonies and tragedies are just as significant as the ecstasies and triumphs. Mourning with a mom who lost her son is just as sacred as celebrating when a neighbor finds a job. Isn't this what Paul's getting at when he urges the Corinthians to be Christ's Body: "If one part suffers, every part suffers with it; if one part is honored, every part rejoices with it." Being the church is about suffering and rejoicing with each other, sharing the agonies and the ecstasies.

& ECSTASY

IT'S THE
SAFEST
SPACE
I'VE EVER
LIVED IN.

- MELISSA McLAMB

A BITTERSWEET

BREAK

As I get ready to leave for Christmas break I realize: I'm going to miss the girls on my team. After three months of never being apart for more than nine hours at a time, two whole weeks will be interesting!

Oh man.

One of the greatest things about this experience has been our house. The *real* late night talks. The dances. The sharing of stories about our days and memories. The back rubs. The hugs. The "I know you're silly, mixed up and don't have it all together but I don't either" laughs and prayers. It's the safest space I've ever lived in.

Tonight we are going out...all of us...downtown.

We will eat Giordano's pizza; sing with an African children's choir at Millennium Park; go ice skating outside; drink German hot chocolate; enjoy one another and *celebrate*.

MISSION YEAR

I've always said that Mission Year ruined my life in a good way. Even now, three years out, with cable television and a car and a life in the suburbs, my life is radically different because of my experience in Atlanta. It took me a while to get over my suburban guilt, I won't lie; but in the end, I decided that Mission Year wasn't meant to make me feel bad about living in the suburbs. It was about exposing me to reality, forcing me to look at society and my individual role in it and making me realize that life is ministry. That's where I am today. Yes, I'm living in Northern Virginia, but I'm carrying on with the ideals of Mission Year: I live and work in the same neighborhood. It's where I shop, where I hang out, where I spend my time. I have a vested interest in my community. Maybe I'm not buddy-buddy with my next door neighbor, but I know this community. I hurt for it. I care about it. I need it to work.

Here's the thing: it's the same community that I was completely unattached to pre-Mission Year. In fact, I loathed this community. But now that I'm back, I can see that God cares for this place, too. God wants to work here, too. And the other thing: it's far from perfect. The problems I learned about in the city are here in the suburbs and, as my particular community experiences a shift in demographics, it's becoming harder and harder to hide these issues.

I'm currently in my third year of teaching, a career that I say I stumbled into by accident, though I know full well this was no accident. I teach at a local public high school where I'm one of ten over-worked and under-paid "World Language" teachers and one of two teachers who work with the Spanish for Native Speakers program. That might give you an idea of the types of kids I work with. In a community that is quickly becoming more anti-Latino, I have the privilege of instilling pride in these children: pride in their culture, in their language, in all that they are and can become.

RUINED MY LIFE

I remember at the closing retreat saying, through tears, that I wanted to do something for "my people." And that's what God has me doing here, in the community I thought I hated. I see the problems of the inner-city here as well: violence, single parents, poverty, gangs. I can still be involved in working for social justice. I can still work one-on-one with these struggling kids and point towards something better, something beyond this reality.

That's Mission Year's legacy. And I really mean that it ruined my life in a good way. Even though at times it sucked and I hated it, Mission Year is the best experience of my life thus far.

WHERE IS

THE JUSTICE?

BLACK ON BLACK

It seems that black men have a lot to overcome in order to get a decent shot at life. I understand the anger that lives within not just black people but within many people of color as we fight against obstacles such as stereotypes, statistics and ignorance.

What I cannot understand is when this anger is turned on other people of color. Gangs turning their anger on one another. Young African American, Latino and Asian men hurting each other over territory in our streets. Territory that, in most cases, they do not even own. It is really sad when such anger is used on each other instead of working together to overcome these obstacles. We witness incredible violence towards people who are, in most cases, in the same situations. People of color should be comparing notes and working together to overcome injustice. We need also to recognize and lock arms with many whites who are our advocates.

I frequent the YMCA in our neighborhood. Last week as I was leaving, three young men tried to sneak in. Many kids from our neighborhood who don't have the money to get memberships try this tactic. The African American man sitting at the desk caught them trying to get in, and the scene unfolded as I came out of the locker room.

The man behind the counter proceeded to tear the hearts out of these young men with insults. He called them criminals, belittled their character and kicked them out of the facility. His last comment: "And don't walk in between the cars. People will think you're trying to break into them and I will call the police." My heart sank. This adult African American male had the opportunity to teach three young men, but his response was to belittle them and to solidify stereotypes.

It felt like the emotional equivalent of black on black crime. His insults were like the bullets of a gun taking the life from some young men. Instead of using this as a time to teach, correct behavior and gain trust, he used it to tear them down. The couple at the desk with me waiting for their ID cards thanked him for dealing with the situation properly. He confidently responded, "Just trying to keep it safe for our members."

Three young men trying to sneak into the Y to play basketball now roam the streets with little to do. Their spirits wounded because even the person who looks like them thinks they are nothing. How safe do you feel? I feel just as safe as I would if I walked into the middle of a drive-by shooting — caught in the crossfire.

ENVIRONMENTAL

I live in an unjust American landscape. The people in my church live in one of Atlanta's urban sacrifice zones. If you sat down to list the social ills that are unequally visited upon my neighborhood, you might be able to name a few of the most prominent. Drug crime, addiction, prostitution, failing schools, broken homes, broken windows, lack of jobs, no public library, adult illiteracy and homelessness would probably come to your mind.

Environmental injustices likely wouldn't appear on your list. When visitors to inner-city Atlanta think about environmental disparities compared to their own neighborhoods, they usually think first about litter. Litter is an environmental problem and it's a sign of social disruption and lack of pride in place. But litter doesn't kill anyone.

Within blocks of our church is a toxic waste facility, a trash transfer station, chemical plants and other facilities that release carcinogens and heavy metals like lead into the air. On almost any environmental index, our area ranks in the worst ten percent of the United States.

The city's huge impoundment lot for towed vehicles occupies the land that would be our neighborhood hub. The collective leaking oil seeping into the unpaved earth beneath these cars pollutes our groundwater and runs off into our streams. The city and county have permitted large freight operations and trucking operations to locate in our neighborhood, bringing with them reckless traffic and concentrated toxic diesel emissions.

Pedestrian fatalities afflict African Americans at a rate two and half times that in the white population in Atlanta, largely because the state Department of Transportation doesn't design roads to accommodate walkers (or cyclists). Hispanic Atlantans are in an even worse plight: concentrated in newer developments but still reliant on walking, they are killed by cars at rates six times higher than whites. These can't be considered

JUSTICE

accidents — they are predictable results of the way we build our cities.

Asthma from air pollution affects large and increasing numbers of kids in my inner-city neighborhood. Nationwide, poor African American children are twice as likely to have asthma as poor white children, and blacks are three times more likely than whites to be killed by asthma. When Atlantans opted for public transportation and telecommuting to reduce traffic congestion for two weeks during the 1996 Olympics, emergency room visits and hospitalizations due to asthma fell by half!

Our neighborhood is one of the worst in the US for lead paint in houses. Nationwide, over 20 percent of black kids in older homes suffer from lead poisoning, compared to just over 5 percent of white kids in older homes. But black kids are also far more likely to live in an older, dilapidated home! In some parts of the country 1 in 3 inner-city children suffers from lead poisoning, which leads to lifelong problems like reduced IQ, slowed body growth, hearing problems, behavioral problems and kidney damage.

Antiquated sewer systems mean that high rainfall events bring floods of wastewater, toilet paper, tampons and condoms through many of our inner-city parks and streets. Dilapidated houses and apartments are havens for rats and roaches (which are themselves triggers for asthma). Landlords, when they decide to treat for these pests, use whatever cheap chemicals they can lay their hands on — often agricultural chemicals not meant to be sprayed indoors.

If you thought harder, you'd realize that greenspace and parks, sidewalks and bike lanes, banks and grocery stores, restaurants and retail are also distributed unequally.

The Bible says we're meant to take a lesson from our environment about

what God is like. Romans 1 says God's eternal power and divine nature should be apparent from the creation.

If kids in my neighborhood were asked to look at metro Atlanta and describe what God is like, I don't think they'd get a vision of Jehovah-Jireh, the God who provides. If all they had to go on was general revelation, their picture of God would be horribly skewed. They would see God's creation as a place that is more threatening to black and Latino families than to whites. Confronted with environmental threats so obviously distributed along ethnic and class lines, they might begin to imagine a racist God.

I must admit that until recently, caring for the environment in whatever form was not on my list of priorities as a Christian. In fact I was quite clueless to any environmental issues up until about seven years ago. It was then that I started to connect what I knew about structural injustice with these environmental issues.

As a black pastor I am part of a history in which pastors not only built the spiritual lives of their congregations by teaching, preaching and living out Christian beliefs, but they also stood for justice against forces that threatened the well-being of their congregations and communities.

These environmental inequities aren't given to us from the hand of an unjust God. They are the results of human sin, a tolerance for injustice unwilling to see or act on the side effects of how we build our cities. I feel I am obligated as a pastor and leader of color to look at this issue and take it as seriously as I do my preaching on Sunday mornings. As we work together to build Dr. King's Beloved Community, we have to think about the words of Jesus in the Lord's Prayer, "Thy kingdom come. Thy will be done, on earth as it is in heaven." I don't believe heaven is a place where people of color have less, so my job is to work that justice throughout this earth.

WHERE IS THE

The church has lost its place in the heart of the neighborhood and not many people seem to care. What used to be the center of the community is now an afterthought to most people, if a thought at all. What has happened to the voice of this powerful institution that has spoken for so many throughout history? How has the influence of the church diminished so much in our time? I don't believe God has decided to back off, so perhaps it is His followers who have decided to retreat.

Perhaps the church has lost its place because its members have forgotten the message and where it is to be promoted. The message of the cross has been lost in the shuffle of time. The message that Jesus died for me in spite of me. Even if I find it within myself to do good things for people, at the end of the day, I am selfish. All my great ideas and intellect can't hide this heart polluted by mean thoughts, rotten attitudes and misplaced pride. If not held accountable, this heart will think and do any number of unpleasant things. Jesus gives life for my garbage. His innocent blood was shed for me and all the guilty. The grace of God through the blood of Jesus makes all the difference. He cures my dirty heart.

That message is to be promoted not just inside the doors of the church but outside. We have let it settle into buildings and pews when it was meant to be lived and proclaimed as good news to the poor. It is captured in the sacrificial offerings made for the poor, outcast and the hungry in our world. It is found in those abolitionists who fought against slavery and in the souls of the students who marched with Dr. King.

The church is to follow the example of Christ: the Word became flesh and made His dwelling among us. Jesus didn't retreat from the hostile world around Him. He moved into our neighborhood.

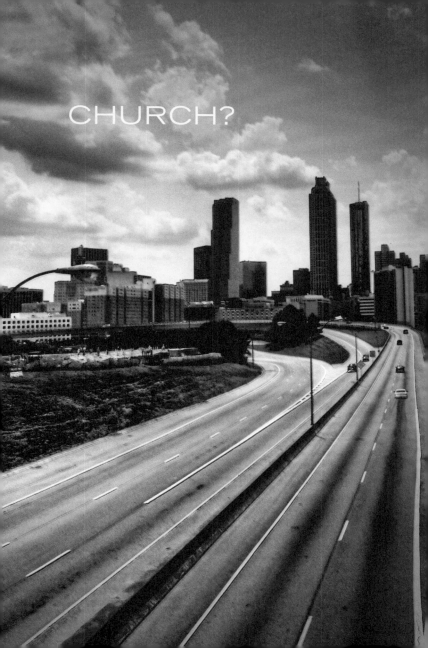

CHURCH?

A SINGLE GARMENT

OF DESTINY

One of the perks of working at Georgia Justice Project is its location directly behind the Martin Luther King, Jr. Center. At least once a week I take a lunch break and just walk around it. It is a great place with the rich history of the civil rights movement and the life of Martin Luther King, Jr. Working in this area encourages me to read up on African American history and I just finished a book by James Cone, *Martin & Malcolm & America*, about Martin Luther King, Jr. and Malcolm X. Both men were great speakers and had great gifts. Martin Luther King, Jr. had this ability, in just a few sentences, to energize, encourage and empower people but at the same time convict and humble people also. There is one quote I read that I feel is a great challenge to our way of thinking and living:

"All men are caught in an inescapable network of mutuality, tied in a single garment of destiny. Whatever affects one directly affects all indirectly. As long as there is poverty in this world, no man can be totally rich even if he has a billion dollars. As long as there is disease rampant and millions of people cannot expect to live more than twenty or thirty years, no man can be totally healthy, even if he just got a clean bill of health from the finest clinic in America. Strangely enough, I can never be what I ought to be until you are what you ought to be. You can never be what you ought to be until I am what I ought to be."

I believe this is what God means when He says to love your neighbor as yourself.

JESUS IS HERE

I headed to Atlanta for my Mission Year just months after walking across a podium and accepting a bachelor's degree which took me four years to earn. I had studied religion. Read the Bible cover to cover. Studied the archeology of Noah's Ark. Debated the history of the early church. Pondered the life that Jesus lived. But within me was a desire for more, a desire to change the world…and with this attitude I arrived in Atlanta.

It didn't take me long to realize that I was in *way* over my head. I had entered into a world that I didn't even know existed. A world where hurt was everywhere. Single moms raising multiple children on limited incomes. Young boys selling drugs to men and women who had been addicted for years and would do anything to score. Alcoholics. Men and women without homes. Shootings. Inadequate schools. Hunger. Loneliness. Anger. Houses falling apart.

Then something happened to me in the midst of all of this. I had always been someone who thought I had it all together, someone who was on the "right path." Suddenly this belief was rocked. It was as if the hopelessness and despair which was all around me was a mirror into my own soul. I began to focus on my own failures and shortcomings…and this was hard. Very hard.

But as time went on something greater happened…amidst all the pain and suffering, I began to experience Jesus. Jesus was here. I didn't doubt this coming in, but I had yet to truly experience the presence of Jesus. I experienced Jesus in my relationships. I got to know a black man who had struggled and was embittered by years of racism. He was a World War II vet and an alcoholic. He was a great friend. I felt Jesus' presence.

I became friends with a young man my age. He was one of the main drug dealers in the neighborhood, going in and out of jail numerous times while I was there. He wanted to change, but knew no other way. I felt Jesus' presence.

I visited a friend in jail who had recently celebrated three months of being clean. His life was coming together but he was arrested for an outstanding warrant from his past. He cried when I visited him because I was the only one who had come. I felt Jesus' presence.

Amongst all the hurt and pain which surrounded me and was inside of me, I felt the presence of Jesus like I never had before. It was good. It was love. And it transformed me. Since leaving Mission Year, I want nothing more and nothing less than to enter the brokenness of life, the brokenness in those around me and within myself. I no longer feel like I have to change the world…Jesus has already done that and is doing it today.

SAFER

When we walked around the neighborhood on Saturday, we prayed at our corner. Circled up, holding hands, I felt the power of God's presence well up in me. As we prayed, my fear of neighborhood drug deals and gun shots flew out of my mind. Holding hands with my team members, I could see the significance of our tall house on the corner of First and Derbigny. We would be a beacon of light in a community infested with drugs and violence. As we said "Amen," we went to talk with a lady on the corner across the street.

Whitney lives across the street from us. She moved in a few months ago and started coming to our church last week. Whitney is in her 50's and can't read, yet she is yearning for more and more of Jesus. "Finding Jesus" was the phrase she used the first time we talked: she wanted me to know that she does indeed know Jesus, but cannot get enough of Him. My heart broke in pieces as she told me she is afraid to go outside and sit on the porch because of the violent activities in the neighborhood. It broke even further when she said she had a Bible in every room of her mold infested house, yet she cannot read the scriptures. I could hardly hold back the tears as she took my hand, grasped it tightly, and thanked us for coming into the neighborhood — as it will make her feel safer to be in the community.

We assured her that we wanted to make sure she made it to church. We wanted to be a part of her life. We wanted to sit and read the Bible to her, since she cannot do it herself. We prayed for her and her fears. She prayed for us and blessed us both.

We saw Whitney in church on Sunday. She was lit up. She didn't sleep the night before because of the activity on our corner, but that didn't stop her from making the trip over to the church.

WHERE IS
THIS IS

THE JUSTICE?
MY JUSTICE.

HE BELIEVED ME

I attended a primarily white Catholic high school in another part of town. One day at school everything began as usual. I was at my locker getting out my books like I did any other morning. For some unknown reason, a white guy named Ralph who I didn't know very well, came up from behind and began choking me. Obviously, he was mad at me about something, though I didn't have a clue what it could be.

"How do you like that, nigger," he growled while he kept his arm locked around my neck and continued to use the word nigger over and over again. The whole incident shocked me so much, I didn't fight back. I couldn't believe it was happening. It felt like I was in some movie scene as he choked me harder and harder.

Some other guys pulled him off me. The hallways were always over full during the change of classes, so there were a lot of people around at the time. When I somehow broke free of his grip, I immediately swung at him and Ralph back at me, until we were in the midst of a big scuffle.

It wasn't long before I found myself sitting in the disciplinarian's office facing a suspension for fighting. I was still angry as I began telling my side of the story: "I was minding my own business when Ralph came up behind me and started choking me. He called me a nigger. You can ask anyone."

Brother John and I were familiar with one another. I'd spent many days in detention for infractions like horsing around or yelling in the hallways, sneaking over to the girls' building, being late for class and starting food fights. The hours I spent in detention could quite possibly have added up to another school year. But Brother John had never seen me angry like this before and had to work hard to calm me down. When he'd finally succeeded, he said, "I believe you, Leroy. If you think you can control yourself, you may return to class and I'll deal with Ralph."

He believed me.

I was shocked. I was prepared for a long drawn out process, Ralph's word versus my word. There was none. I couldn't wrap my mind around this experience. All the time I spent seeing the school primarily as racist. The many days of complaining that we were being forced to do what the white people wanted. All the awkward conversations and jokes about race I had endured. Add to that this recent experience of some crazy white guy calling me a nigger for no apparent reason. Now this white man believed me without question or hesitation.

I didn't stop to think about it then, but Brother John and his faith in me at that moment has come back many times when I would unfairly judge one white person by the acts of another. Because that day one white person was an extreme racist and the other an unquestioning, fully supportive friend. The lines had become blurry. Black and white became gray. In between hate and punishment was a place for brotherhood and peace in the form of simple trust.

MONSTERS

I was never really afraid of the dark when I was a kid, but I do remember being concerned when the lights went off. I knew there was no monster in my closet that was going to jump out, but the darkness gave me a little pause. This would usually lead to some reflection on my part, which ended in a quick talk with God. Off to sleep I would go with the belief that even if the monster was there, he was no match for my parents or for God so I was safe.

I wish the darkness that I find myself in everyday were as easy to get over. Here the monsters are real. Poverty, poor educational systems, domestic violence, substandard housing, predatory lending, prostitution, homelessness, lack of community, greed and racism. These monsters are not hiding in the closet. They are out in the open.

I'm not afraid, but I am very concerned. As I look around at Christians, it seems we are walking in darkness ignoring the monsters that are wreaking havoc all around us. As followers of Jesus, I don't think we should be afraid but we should be concerned and that concern should cause us to pause. Hopefully, our pause leads to reflection and reflection takes us to the words of Jesus, "You are the light of the world."

The monsters are there, but they are no match for the light. The good that is of God is far more than evil can handle. My problem is that sometimes I feel too safe and go off to sleep. Sleep in my comfortable house or church or with my group of friends, while evil destroys the world and people around me.

So many Christians living safe lives, knowing the darkness is no match for the light, unafraid of the monsters that circle about, content to do nothing but sleep.

Sweet Dreams.

JOHN 3:19-21 (THE MESSAGE)

This is the crisis we're in: God-light streamed into the world, but men and women everywhere ran for the darkness. They went for the darkness because they were not really interested in pleasing God. Everyone who makes a practice of doing evil, addicted to denial and illusion, hates God-light and won't come near it, fearing a painful exposure. But anyone working and living in truth and reality welcomes God-light so the work can be seen for the God-work it is.

OUR DEEPEST FEAR
IS NOT THAT WE ARE
INADEQUATE. OUR
DEEPEST FEAR IS THAT
WE ARE POWERFUL
BEYOND IMAGINATION.
IT IS OUR LIGHT MORE
THAN OUR DARKNESS
WHICH SCARES US. WE
ASK OURSELVES — WHO
ARE WE TO BE BRILLIANT,
BEAUTIFUL, TALENTED,
AND FABULOUS. BUT
HONESTLY, WHO ARE YOU
TO NOT BE SO?

- MARIANNE WILLIAMSON

SEPARATE

It is a widely publicized fact that the majority of public schools in urban America have been failing for a long time. My neighborhood is no exception. At one time our elementary, middle and high schools were all on the needs improvement list. That means that a child growing up in our neighborhood could go through school and have a sub-par education by no fault of her own. As a follower of Jesus who believes that every child is created in the image of God, this is unacceptable.

One solution many Christians have advocated over the years is developing Christian schools. I have worked in Christian schools and have even started one here in Atlanta. I am an advocate of Christian education as a partial solution, but not at the expense of an entire system that leaves children behind at alarming numbers.

Christian education has offered parents a viable option in a less than adequate situation. But I have also witnessed Christian schools being used as a place for the wealthy and for Christians to "protect" their children. In fact, the growth of "Christian" schools began to increase around the time of desegregation. People were protecting their children from black people. There are exceptions. I have also seen urban Christian schools which encourage diversity and have sliding scales so that any parent can afford it. These schools have provided a successful alternative for many cities around the country, but I think we can do more as Christians. We can make it a goal to change the system.

Schools are neighborhood based; therefore, they can still be influenced by a group of intentional citizens. Every year, a few schools within the public school system somehow manage to become excellent in educating children. This is achieved through parent involvement and community partnerships. A group of neighbors living in the same place raising their children together can change the outlook of a school. Instead of continuing the legacy of separate and unequal, let's

& UNEQUAL

make an effort to change the system for the good of all the children.

Jesus told us, "You are the salt of the earth; you are the light of the world." Why can't that salt and light reach into a neighborhood school, a school district and maybe even into the entire public school system?

ESPERANZA

Esperanza. This is one of the most beautiful sounding words I think I could roll off my tongue. It is Spanish for hope, which is the biggest thing God has taught and shown me in Little Village this year. The people I work with, my roommates, the beloved students at Social Justice High School, my church: these are the people that encapsulate what hope really means. Going through hard situations, losing people you love to shootings or deportations and still loving people and God without holding anything back — that is hope. Lately, I am learning the most about hope from the students I see every day at SoJo High. I love them as if they were my own brothers and sisters. They're more real and genuine than any inner-city kid stereotype you know of. Forget about *Freedom Writers, Dangerous Minds* and *Hardball*. This is what these kids are really like:

First, there's Bryan. Here I am working in the In School Suspension Room and Bryan comes in with a pass from his teacher. He didn't get in trouble; he just wanted to come to do his work. I was so confused about why someone would choose to come here. He sweetly, but sincerely, told me, "I get off task sometimes in class and just want to talk to people. I know when I get in those moods, it's better for me to come here where I'll be more focused and actually get my work done." My heart warms because I know he means every word of it. Whenever I see Bryan, he asks me about how I got a Psychology degree. Bryan really wants to help people, to be a counselor, and would be awesome at it. He is a total athlete but he breaks all the stereotypes by being incredibly philosophical, sensitive and caring as well.

Then there's Amber. She's short and has waist length brown hair with bright blonde streaks. She makes up for her physical smallness with her huge smile, which makes her stand a head above the rest. Amber oozes with sincere friendliness and warmth; no matter how hard a person is, they can keep no guard up around her. She's one of the girls

I have been training to be a mentor next year. Lots of girls look up to her because she is not only pretty; she also has a beautiful personality, maturity and realness about her. When I said hi to her during passing periods, she came up to me and gave me a huge hug that I didn't expect at all. It was my best surprise all day.

These kids are indestructible to me. No matter who gets shot, who gets into a fight or who gets involved with gangs, these students keep going. They keep loving me and others around them. They live life to the fullest and don't let any loss keep them from living. God is totally present here and shows me His hope in their excited eyes every day.

"I guess when I think about the last year, the images

that come to mind are just people's faces: faces of my

neighbors, co-workers, patients at the health center,

smiling, dancing people at the senior center and a herd

of kids on my block sprinting into my arms and yelling my

name at the top of their lungs."

PHILLY TEAM MEMBER 2006-2007

TEARS OF LOVE

I knew I would miss my kids from Camden before I even left, but I never imagined that I would be so emotional about it. I was asked by the pastor of my parents' church to say a few words about the past four months I've spent in Camden. I told about the last full day I spent in Camden sorting, packaging and delivering Christmas gifts that had been donated to our camp kids.

As I talked about one family in particular, I had to stop several times to choke back tears. Normally, I am all about crying. I don't try to hold it in, but I knew if I let myself go, I would not be able to utter intelligible words and the congregation would just be lost in a sea of sobs and mumbles. I was not sad. Not at all. My heart was simply too full of love and passion for the kids I was talking about to hold it all inside. My tears were the overflow of my heart.

I told the congregation that I was frustrated because I knew that whatever words I spoke would never fully explain the kids I work with. My words can never paint a picture that will sufficiently explain to others how my heart is attached to these kids and this city I have been living in. But, what I am doing in this city is no more difficult or important than things that can be done anywhere.

There are kids everywhere who need someone to be a role model for them. To listen to them talk about their new crush. To watch them sing and dance. To tell them they are capable of behaving and capable of having lasting and meaningful relationships. To be one of those lasting and meaningful relationships. All it takes is time, commitment, love and intentionality. For some people, their part in loving kids is to send Christmas gifts. For others, it is to tutor them once a week for an hour. It doesn't matter what part you play, as long as you are acting as part of the Body in some manner. The Body is the most beautiful thing when all the parts are working differently, but together, for the same goal.

TERRIFIED

In two weeks I have to move out of the place I've called home for the past year. It doesn't seem possible the life I was terrified of living is now the life I'm terrified of losing. The streets I was afraid to walk down, the people I thought I was never going to understand, the girls I thought were never going to give me any alone time — all of these have changed in my perspective. They've all become people and places I will never be able to forget, will have an extremely difficult time walking away from and will always be in debt to for teaching me life lessons I would never have been able to learn elsewhere.

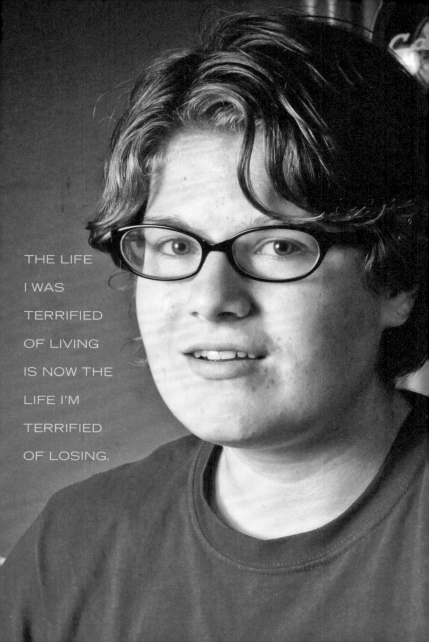

THE LIFE
I WAS
TERRIFIED
OF LIVING
IS NOW THE
LIFE I'M
TERRIFIED
OF LOSING.

WHERE DO I

BEGIN?

TWO STONES

"I have been to the mountaintop, and I have seen the Promised Land. I may not get there with you, but mine eyes have seen the glory of the coming of the Lord."

I have often wondered what Dr. King saw on that mountaintop. What did the Promised Land look like? Did Dr. King see people? Did he see buildings? Were there trees and flowers? What did people wear? Did everyone walk? Whatever he saw, it must have been incredible. When he later spoke of that vision, it flowed from him like fire and caused the world to change.

I sometimes think the fire we saw in Dr. King was a combination of the faith nurtured in him and the injustice he saw all around him. The two rubbed together like two stones creating sparks in his soul. Every time he saw or experienced injustice, it rubbed up against his faith, generating sparks. Eventually those sparks started an uncontrollable fire.

If this is the case, then you and I can also experience the mountaintop. The key might be letting our faith rub up against injustice. Let's give it a try.

30,000 kids die each day from starvation.

Rub that against this:
"When I was hungry you fed me, when I was thirsty you gave me something to drink, when I was a stranger you welcomed me, when I was naked you gave me clothes, when I was sick or in prison you visited me...When you have done it for the least of my brothers and sisters you have done it for me." (Matthew 25:35-36,40)

There are homeless men, women and children living on streets in every major city in this country.

Rub that against this:
Is this not the worship I have chosen...to loose the chains of injustice, and to free those who are oppressed? (Isaiah 58:6)

Urban public schools are failing kids everyday.

Rub that against this:
Sitting down, Jesus called the Twelve and said, "If anyone wants to be first, he must be the very last, and the servant of all." He took a little child and had him stand among them. Taking him in his arms, he said to them, "Whoever welcomes one of these little children in my name welcomes me; and whoever welcomes me does not welcome me but the one who sent me." (Mark 9:35-37)

Daily, senior citizens fall victim to predatory lenders and lose their homes.

Rub that against this:
Pure religion and undefiled before the Father is this: to visit the fatherless and widows in their affliction and to keep oneself unspotted from the world. (James 1:27)

Do you feel the passion, the heat starting to ignite in your soul? Dr. King lit a fire that still has not been extinguished. The passion he showed toward other people and against injustice because of his faith lives today. How do we join with Dr. King to fan the fire instead of allowing it to go out? How do we let the gospel message rub up against injustice in our neighborhood? What will it take to create a fire in us that compels us to act?

Faith and injustice. Pick up two stones and start rubbing.

Sooner or later, when a group of people get together the subject of money comes up. American society depends on money. Money, who has it and what we do with it are significant issues. Run DMC, a popular 80's rap group, sang:

> *Money is the key to end all your woes*
> *Your ups, your downs, your highs and your lows*
> *Won't you tell me the last time that love bought you clothes?*

Money is seen as the way to get what you want in life. People without money want it; those with money protect it. We know it can't cure cancer, but some would argue that it gets you better doctors. It won't protect you from anything, but it buys you a more secure place to live.

Yet another step up from having money is having wealth. Wealth accumulates when a family member has made and kept so much money that it will stay in a family for generations to come through trust funds, wills, endowments, etc. This is more than just money; it is ongoing financial security for generations. The person born into wealth doesn't need to worry about earning money, he simply chooses how to spend the money he's been given.

Because of the way the world we live in works, those with money and wealth get power accordingly. Little money, little power. Some money, some power. A lot of money, a lot of power. Wealth, incredible power and influence. This plays out in many areas in our society. Consider the possible participants in a neighborhood meeting. A renter in a subsidized housing apartment may have a voice, but very little power. A neighborhood store owner has some power. But if Wal-Mart sends a representative, everyone is listening. Imagine if a member of the Hilton family showed up. He would be introduced by name and given a seat of honor. The renter can join everyone else

FRIEND WITH MONEY

in the folding chairs. People are treated accordingly based on the amount of money and or wealth they have.

What does a New Neighbor do with money? What do I do with the money I have? How do I respond to a person who has money when I don't? Some have advocated that those with money should just hand it out so those who need it can just receive it. This is one solution, but all I've seen that lead to is the givers getting burned out and the receivers losing dignity. This is an incredible place to create relationships. An opportunity for those who follow Jesus to rise above the patterns of this world. To rethink what money is for and how to use it to our advantage as neighbors.

Humans were created in the image of the Creator. We could decide to follow Him by creating. What if we combined our money and our relationships to create new ventures? The homeless and the wealthy could collaborate together as neighbors to bring life to a community. Ministry donors and parents of the children sending kids to the neighborhood "ministry" could work together for education solutions. We could start by talking to our neighbors, hear about the problems and potentials from every perspective and dream together about what could be. Then we could start creating.

God created the whole world, but he started humanity with just one man and woman. We could follow Him by starting small. Invest in local people and ventures with proven leaders in the neighborhood to create positive environments for people to thrive. Don't just invest in the biggest or most polished around you. The YMCA and the Boys and Girls Clubs are great, but they are not the only things to support. Ms. Jane's after school program or Father John's soup kitchen serve in unique ways as well. Neighborhood thrift shops that hire teens that live in the neighborhood and coffee shops that train young people need our support.

We could decide to only invest in and patronize programs that use this model. Programs that encourage the kind of leadership that gives every person an equal voice and pays particular attention to those who understand the unique needs of a particular neighborhood. This would be a new way to harness the power of money. We could use our money, our voices, our power, our love toward moving people to work together. This could build a new neighborhood.

HOPE VS.

I was raised in a church where hope was the order of the day. My family was not rich. In fact, we struggled quite a bit financially as my mother worked to raise four boys. There was injustice all around, but there was hope. It was preached from the pulpit on Sunday and lived out in my mother each day as she prayed and sang God's praises before me. My school teachers used it as motivation and Bible teachers pumped it into my spirit. The older saints, as we called them, prayed about it each week at prayer meeting and the deacons hummed it in their prayers.

Hope.

Hope for a better day or hope that God would meet the day's need. Hope that there was a God and that He cared deeply for me and would make up for the pain and injustice I saw around me each day. In fact, I've learned more about hope from older people who have lived through racism and injustice firsthand than I have from privileged

CYNICISM

people who have rarely struggled in their lives. I am beginning to think that cynicism might be a luxury only the privileged can entertain. For those not privileged by race or power or money, hope is what you rely on for life. I have seen hope work in my life. But still I turn from it much too often.

I turn to cynicism.

Cynicism has taken the place in my heart where hope used to reign. I am still a dreamer, but I have compromised my dreams for cynicism more often than I care to admit these days. Cynicism floats around in my head as I look at the conditions of my neighborhood or if I think about the environment or the fact that so many of my brothers are in jail. I often spout off about what the "church" is or is not doing and how I think that Christians are falling short of the mark that Jesus set. I often justify my cynicism as being a critical thinker. The truth is that cynicism works like a poison, destroying your spirit. It consumes your eyes, your mind and your heart with the problems.

But hope is different. Hope sees a future. Hope connects your life to a bigger purpose. Some would say that hope lacks substance, that it is a tool of the weak. But positive change cannot happen for a person in poverty or of less privilege if there is no hope. Hope is always the fuel for change; it refreshes the heart of weary people and gives strength to the oppressed. It is a reason to persevere in struggle. In fact, hope may be a sign of strength, an instrument of the brave. Romans 5 declares, "We also rejoice in our sufferings, because we know that suffering produces perseverance; perseverance, character; and character, hope. And hope does not disappoint us, because God has poured out His love into our hearts by the Holy Spirit."

With this kind of hope, we will not be disappointed.

REBUILDING

As we drove along the Gulf Coast highway through towns like Long Beach, Ocean Springs and Pass Christian on our way to Gulfport, Mississippi, I could not believe my eyes. Such total destruction: buildings left in rubble, mansions completely flattened. At first, I was overwhelmed with thoughts of God's power: a strong hand that could command the winds and waters to bring such devastation. I questioned my role in responding to this devastation. I wondered what His reasons were for bringing on this storm. I honestly questioned Him: "God, since You brought this on, do You just want it to stay this way?"

God met me in these thoughts of sadness and confusion and reminded me that His is a story of continuous hope and redemption. Every instance of destruction comes with an opportunity for rebuilding. From Adam to Noah to Nehemiah to Lazarus to Jesus — God has been bringing life and hope out of desperate situations. God is providing us, His people, an opportunity to respond to this disaster in love. We are called to be His hands and feet, and that is why I am excited to join in rebuilding the Gulf Coast. It won't be easy and it won't always be pleasant, but worth it? Definitely.

ONE MORE THING

With the number of Chicago student lives being lost to gun violence rapidly increasing, there has been a parallel in rising concern for our community's safety. My supervisor at Hope House, Stanley, shared the concern and felt led to call a series of "Fast, Pray and March" outings here in North Lawndale.

A couple weeks ago I walked into the office and Stanley said, "Girl, we got work to do. We're going to do a prayer march. Actually, 10 marches." Then he showed me a PowerPoint presentation that he put together that morning with all the details. I was shocked to say the least, but knew that Stanley meant business. So I helped him fancy up the PowerPoint presentation, then made 50 copies for him and he went on his way, visiting every pastor he knew in North Lawndale to get them to join us in our efforts.

That was about two weeks ago. Since then we've sent out emails, posted flyers, held a community planning meeting, had five churches commit to participating, met with the Police Department, had a news media press conference, spoken with politicians and talked with local stores to get food donations. And wow, this stuff gets tiring!

But it has been so amazing working with Stanley, just seeing how God has laid this vision on his heart. He's not a community organizer, he just felt called to see the community coming together, publicly declaring they *care* about the community and are willing to march and pray in the streets to let people know it. The man already has three different job titles: Director of Hope House, a transitional recovery home for men; Director of Celestial Ministries, a music program for kids whose parents have been incarcerated; and Minister of Music for Lawndale Community Church. He does not need to be doing any more! But he just felt God nudging him to do this, so he did.

I have so much to learn. I don't know how or why or even if I am cut out to be such an obedient and Spirit-led servant of God. I still struggle with this daily. But, I am so grateful for this opportunity to be working under obedient, faithful servants like Stanley.

BROWNIES

One Saturday I visited Janelle, a sweet woman with five children, a loving husband and a beautiful home that lives a block from us. They were celebrating her youngest daughter's 23rd birthday and invited my teammates and I to come. From the time we first met Janelle, she was nothing but loving to us and opened her home to us to truly make us part of her family. We sat around her living room until 10:30 p.m. just talking and watching *Ice Age* in Spanish. I'm proud to say I learned a few new phrases.

I was looking around at Janelle and her family, so comfortably talking and laughing with us, and thought back to how we first met her. Our second week in Chicago my teammate and I, in all our awkwardness, made brownies, covered them with foil and went on a walk around our neighborhood to introduce ourselves to neighbors. We met Janelle, who was wearing a bright purple shirt and was having a garage sale. She and her youngest son, Denis, loved the brownies. Last night I found it funny that such a simple thing, a plate of brownies, brought us to such a great relationship with her and her family. God really shows up in the little things. We think that in order to give or receive God's love we have to do great, profound things. But I'm realizing, more here than ever, that Jesus was about the simple acts and seeing how God is present in even the simplest of conversations or the smallest of victories.

"We can do no great things. Only small things with great love."

MOTHER THERESA

WHERE DO I
THIS

BEGIN?

IS MY BEGINNING.

O FATHER,

I still remember when my father left home. For a few weeks I felt numb. The life I had known was over. I struggled to get my head around the idea that home would never be the same again. I tried not to think about the fact that dad would never live with us again. This was so painful that I shut down emotionally. No one could come in. Leroy Barber was closed.

WHERE ART THOU?

My heart was no longer available. The pain put me in major survival mode, and that meant protecting my feelings at all times. I developed an outer shell that was very hard to penetrate. I looked like a wonderful, caring person on the outside, but I could care less most of the time. I dealt with this hurt internally so people would never know if I didn't care, nor could they help me out of my internal darkness. I just suffered silently as I established shallow relationships and engaged in harmful behavior.

The statistics for children growing up without fathers in their home reveal that many more children are closed as well.

> 63% of youth suicides are from fatherless homes.
> 85% of all youth in prison grew up in a fatherless home.
> 71% of all high school dropouts come from a fatherless home.
> 85% of all children that exhibit behavioral disorders come from fatherless homes.

It is now my conviction that part of being a good neighbor includes seeing myself as a dad to the children living around me. In order to open that part of a child's heart, they need the love of a father. Every child longs for a father's voice in their lives. A father who spends time with them building memories. A father who demonstrates love in words, deeds and lifestyle. A father willing to give direction with solid "why" answers to the questions of life. A father who plants convictions in the hearts of children by modeling integrity, faithfulness, humility and faith.

I have done this for my children and get twice the joy by being "Poppa Leroy" in the neighborhood. Pastors, teachers, youth leaders and yes, even neighbors, must fill the role of father that is missing in so many lives. Many children are looking for Dad. We can help them find him.

PRESIDENT

My office is located just two blocks from my home in Atlanta. I have the great privilege of walking there and back everyday. I also have a backyard trampoline which serves as a popular spot for neighborhood young people after school. While walking home from the office one afternoon I ran into one of these young men on his way to the same destination, my back yard.

"What's up, Z?"

"Hey, Mr. Leroy, can we play on the trampoline?"

I had anticipated this question.

"Sure, Z, let me get in from work and settle for a few minutes and then you can come by."

"Where do you work, Mr. Leroy?"

I thought about giving him my Mission Year spiel: I work for a ministry that recruits young adults from all around the United States to do a year of service in an urban neighborhood. We link them with a local church. They do community service and neighborhood outreach in an effort to represent Jesus. Instead I said, "I am president of an organization that works with young adults in Philly, Chicago, New Orleans and here."

"You are a President?!" He seemed to be really impressed by this, but then confused. "Then why do you walk to work and let us play on your trampoline? Shouldn't people be driving you around and you live in a big house somewhere else?"

I replied, "I am not that kind of President."

"Good. I like coming over to play on the trampoline. I want to be a president and have a trampoline so kids can come over to play."

Off and running went Z, which was good because I could not control my tears.

Quite often I find myself in conversations about the plight of children growing up in a neighborhood like the one in which I live, where there is high crime, substandard housing and poor schools. I often wonder how children like Z will get a healthy vision for their future. But with one five minute conversation and an ordinary backyard trampoline, a 10 year old can imagine a bright future that includes sharing with his neighbors. I could not have planned the moment any better.

I pray I see Z on my walk home more often.

A WORD ON HOPE

Hope is a funny word. It forces us to think positively in the midst of chaos. Hope tells us to believe in good no matter what things look like. Hope puts a positive spin on suffering, and pushes us to believe when there is plenty of evidence not to. A doctor's prognosis, the bank's final answer, a teacher's declaration of failure. Hope pushes back on us when we are down and offers a way out.

It seems to be that hope plants itself in particularly profound ways in the hearts of those that suffer most among us. It sings in the heart of the oppressed, laughs in the soul of the outcast, quiets the mind of the outsider and expands the vision of the humble. Hope even brings life to dead things.

There is a down side to hope. It leaves us dry when it sees self-reliance and flees in the face of cynicism. It is not invincible, but needs an open heart to flourish in. Hope hides itself in the corner when fear and worry make their way into our hearts. Hope can only stay alive if it has a host. A soul to feed it, a believing heart in the midst of despair. This is when it kicks in and takes over the mind and soul like smog over a city in the summer. You can't always see it, but you know it's there because you feel it in your lungs when you take a breath.

You can't escape it when it's loose. Every breath you take, it enters your psyche and takes over. You start to believe. To expect good. To see good. Your language changes. Your passion ignites. Hope takes over. God is present.

Mission Year changed how I view my role as a follower of Christ in this world. Mission Year taught me that my life is my ministry, that I must be an active participant in the world around me and be intentional about having an impact on my little corner of it.

At the grocery store, I see a young mom with a baby and a screaming child. I can feel her frustration and anxiety. I offer to walk through the grocery store with her, push her cart, grab items off the shelf or entertain her child. All she needs is a little help, some calm, a life line to grab for a minute.

At the coffee shop, someone sits down at my table. I put away my book, smile and ask about his day. I hear this person's life story, some heartache and trouble as well, and I just listen. I try to let him know that he is important, that someone cares.

An incident in my community sparks racial tension. I find out all I can about it. I attend the community meetings that strive for healing, I participate in the conversations and I try to be as vulnerable and honest as possible.

I see someone sitting alone at the back of the sanctuary on Sunday. I ask if I can sit by her. I can see her wariness and discomfort so I try to make my church feel like home.

I participate in the discussions I hear around me about the church, our country, the world; and I listen to the opinions of those around me. I vote. I recycle and try to use less energy. I volunteer where I am out of my comfort zone and try to learn from the people I meet there.

The people I talk to throughout my day; the relationships I cultivate; the causes I believe in and support; my response to current issues; in

A NEW WAY OF LIVING

every little aspect of my daily life. I constantly encounter opportunities to love God and love people, to be a Samaritan kind of neighbor and, because of Mission Year, I recognize them as such. It is my responsibility to act on these opportunities whenever and however I can. I fail a lot, but I keep trying — Mission Year taught me that as well.

I met the Robertsons one night while delivering meals with the Salvation Army in our neighborhood. When I met them they were battling through issues with the Social Security office because nearly all of their income had been unexpectedly cut off. They asked if I might be able to help them out. I said yes, not really knowing what I could do.

THE GIFT OF FRIENDS

I began to visit them regularly on my walk home from school. It was during my afternoon visits that I began to get to know who they were and how they wound up in the Pittsburgh neighborhood of Atlanta. I learned that both Jan and Aaron suffered from mental and severe physical disabilities. Both had narrowly escaped abusive relationships and dangerous family situations. Both diabetics, they needed a combined 44 prescription medications to be able to survive and function. They came to Atlanta because they heard rents were cheaper here.

What struck me the most about the Robertsons was their optimism amidst seemingly bleak circumstances. Their life basically consisted of making it to and from doctor appointments on public transportation. They lived in a tiny one-room apartment that the landlord neglected and barely kept up to code. They knew no one in Atlanta and had no friends or family in the area. It would have been so easy for the Robertsons to feel sorry for themselves. But I never got that from them. All I ever got was warmth, optimism and gratitude. They were so glad to have each other. They were glad to have a roof over their heads. They were glad to have (just barely) enough money to eat. And, as they constantly reminded me, they were glad to have me as their friend.

God really stretched me through my yearlong friendship with the Robertsons. Through our trips to the grocery store, afternoons at the local laundromat, dinners at my house and even in our occasional episodes at the emergency room together, they always reminded me of what it means to give thanks in all circumstances. They would often say that God was looking out for them when He brought me to their doorstep. What I could never really explain to them was what a gift God had given me through my friendship with them.

PLAYING IT SAFE

What is it about American culture that has us convinced we have "arrived" once we are completely independent? Our collective mentality seems to be that to have any sort of dependence on anyone or anything is a sign of weakness. Whether that dependence is in the work place, in our neighborhoods or in our friendships and/or families, we have convinced others that we don't need them, and even worse, we have convinced ourselves. This can end up leaving us feeling lonely, depressed and, worst of all, empty because we think we should have this feeling of "making it," but it turns out making it alone isn't such an amazing feeling.

Luckily for us, God gives us a bit of an advantage through the truth of the Bible. Those pages are filled with directives to be in relationship. With God. With others. But it seems to me that many of us still seem to be missing the point. In today's culture, even if one believes in the God of the Bible, it's easy to lose the relationships of faith to the morality of religion.

It is not always easy to pour oneself into and invest in others. That is definitely one thing I have learned this year. It is not always convenient and you do not always have the energy it takes. One thing I can say for sure: truly loving others means taking risks. Especially when you may not have much in common with the people you are trying to get to know. You can't be sure your efforts will be well received or the person will appreciate you for who you are. It can be a bit scary to put yourself out there. However, when I think back on the last 9+ months and look at all the friendships I have formed, from roommates to neighbors, I wonder: if risks were not taken, would there be much to show for those relationships now?

I can't say for sure. And I know there are definitely times that I could have risked more. If there's one thing I've learned about myself it's how guarded I can be when it comes to building relationships, but I think realizing this about myself is half the battle. And even though I'm not sure what realizing this fact means for my life, I know I want to take risks, as difficult as that might be at times. I don't want to "play it safe" and miss out on relationships from which I can learn and grow.

WHAT DO I BRING?

SONS

I was 12 years old. My father had picked up a girlfriend and a cocaine habit. My mom was left to raise three boys alone. One evening, after our lights and water had been turned off, my mom sat with us boys and read the Psalms to us. She wept, obviously grieved by the situation we were in. I can only imagine losing your husband and dignity as well. But as she read, something miraculous occurred. I felt an overwhelming sense of being loved by her and God. I knew I was cared for despite the fact that our family had nothing and I was embarrassed to face my friends.

That is the moment when I realized that God could heal. I learned that my well-being wasn't dependent upon what things looked like around me. Through my Mom, I somehow tapped into God. He calmed me through my mom. I became aware that He was right in the room with me and wanted to be. I've never forgotten that moment.

We look for answers to so many questions by reading books and going to so-called wise people. We seek out answers from big name speakers or teachers who come to us via the media. We flock to big revivals and conventions in droves. Yet God says, "I am in the small things." God says, "Be still and know that I am God." The Bible tells us, "When we are weak then He is strong." "The heavens declare His glory."

In one of the most profound moments of my life, through the prayer and meditation of a woman who had been left by her husband in a dark, cold house, there was God. Loud and clear with incredible comfort. He spoke. He wrapped his arms around a mom and her three sons and I was forever changed.

LIVING

I believe that every dedicated family following Jesus is a great instrument for the Kingdom of God. A family serving together is a picture of God's love and grace.

My family has been the greatest part of my life. Donna, Jessica, Josh and Joel have been an incredible blessing to me. They have also been my most committed partners in ministry. They have been through all the ups and downs that come with the life we have chosen to live. A life where we have said we would answer God's call first without compromise. Donna was there as I struggled with leaving a regular paying job in 1989 to pursue ministry. Jess was two years old at the time and went with us each night to give out clothes and food to homeless people living on the streets of Philadelphia. Josh and Joel

TOGETHER

have provided free labor. From the time they could lift a hand to help they participated in several building projects, cleaned up after numerous events and served countless meals. Together, we have birthed several ministries: Restoration Ministries, Atlanta Youth Academies, Community Fellowships After-school Enrichment Program and Summer Day Camps, Mission Year Atlanta and Atlanta Community Fellowships Church. A family is a powerful tool in God's hands.

The influence of a family, though, is seen in more than just the programs and ministries they do together. Our best moments in life and ministry are when life and ministry are one. When you can't tell if this is ministry or just life. When I sit on the sofa watching football and some teens from the neighborhood stop by and join me. When my kids and the neighbor kids are playing in the yard and making too much noise and I tell everyone to be quiet. My wife, Donna likes to cook on Thanksgiving. She naturally includes any kids who want to help. Our house is always open and there are always people there. This means they see the good and the bad. They see how our family relates to one another in positive ways and sometimes through the conflict. I don't know if that's ministry or just life at this point, but one thing I do know is that we are a family trying to live out our values. We want to be more than just people doing the task of ministry. We want to be good neighbors by sharing our lives with the people around us.

525,600 MINUTES

I am often asked what can be done in a year. "Can it really make a difference? It seems like such a short time. To be truly effective, you need to make a long-term commitment." My daily life reminds me that the challenges of poverty and race will take much longer than a year to solve. These situations are massive and need consistent attention. It's a good thing we are doing just that.

Every year we get a new group of faithful young people to commit to serving God in the city. Those young people join in a long line of committed followers of Jesus. It seems that too often we detach the work of the ministry as our own work, as if the work you and I engage in is not connected to anything else. We have put the value of individualism onto the gospel. We see ministry as simply "my work." What can I accomplish in one year? What difference will our team make in this city this year? We focus only on the present moment when it is, in fact, God's work that He promised to continue until He returns. When we join God in the work He is doing, we live in His time and His reality.

As we join God's work, we stand back and see the difference that just one year can make.

A year is a building block for the future. Getting an education is very important and fundamental to many things in life. How do you get that education? One year at a time, each year building on the others. Third grade can seem irrelevant if you only look at third grade. When high school algebra comes along, suddenly that multiplication you learned in Mr. Hamilton's third grade class becomes invaluable. One year builds on another.

A year offers countless opportunities to interact with other people. Consider the influence of some people you've met on your journey. A teacher that made a difference, a class that changed your perspective, a lecture that jolted you. While I agree that long-term relationships are what shape us over time, people come in and out of our lives for a brief season and have a profound impact. A science teacher that is passionate about science and connects with the kid who was made to be a scientist. This teacher creates a place for born scientists to discover not just a future, but themselves.

A year holds the promise of a drastically changed life. You fall in love in a year and commit to spend the rest of your life together. You learn to play an instrument and it lifts you to be a musician. You teach for the first time and it captures your heart. You nail that first jump shot, hit that first homerun, paint your first work of art.

In one year on the streets of Philly, Atlanta, Chicago, New Orleans, Wilmington or Camden someone's life can be changed forever by a passionate follower of Jesus living, serving, loving, advocating and praying for their neighbors. Mission Year team members join God's eternal work in the 525,600 minutes they are given.

What are you doing with your 525,600 minutes to make every one of them count?

"I have experienced God in many ways and met His people and seen His work, which goes beyond my time in the city. He is bigger than I am, He preceded me into the city and will remain after I leave, and He continues to do good work through His people there."

PHILLY TEAM MEMBER 2006-2007

FINDING

I met Filipa in January when I was asked to accompany her to the hospital. She was a student in ESL classes a friend of mine taught. Her English wasn't very good and she was worried that she wouldn't be able to understand the doctor.

Filipa and I arrived 15 minutes early for her appointment and proceeded to wait three and a half hours. We made polite conversation, discussing the intricacies of languages and the difficulties we faced in learning them. By the third hour we had exhausted that topic and had begun to share about our families, our homes and anything else I could express in Spanish. At last, her name was called. During the visit, I translated what I could and used a dictionary for what I couldn't.

FAMILY

Everything went smoothly. As we parted ways, Filipa asked if I would come to her home for dinner. I accepted and accepted again every Thursday afternoon from then until the end of my Mission Year.

Each Thursday I shared a meal with Filipa, her husband and her two daughters. They opened their home and their lives to me: inviting me to Baptisms, birthday parties, graduations and, ultimately, to participate in a ceremony in which Filipa and Marco renewed their wedding vows. What meant most, though, was the way they allowed me into their daily lives. We did homework. We watched movies when we were sick. We picked the girls up from school. We walked the dog. We spent time downtown. And we sat for long hours at the kitchen table discussing whatever issues arose: big or small, happy or sad.

My family back home means everything to me. Leaving my family for this faraway city was a difficult decision. However, God, in His infinite love and grace, provided for me. Filipa, Marco, Estella and Graciela became my family here. When I missed my own family or felt lonely, I had only to go to Filipa's house to remember that I was cared for and why I love being Mexican. They reminded me of who I am and where I come from. They challenged me in how I view myself and encouraged me to be exactly who I am.

"I LOVE YOU"

One of the best friends I made here is a guy named Akeem. To even attempt to explain the incredible nature of this man would be a grave injustice to all that he is and represents. Therefore, the best I can do is simply to give you a few bullet points. Akeem means "humble servant" and his work ethic reflects just that. He works the shower and laundry facilities at the shelter and has been living out of an abandoned apartment building with several other people for a few years now. He's always the first one to say hello to me in the morning with a huge smile and hug, and constantly tries to make me feel guilty when I have to leave at the end of the day.

On my day off last week, I saw Akeem with his girlfriend, Porsha, walking through downtown Camden. I ran up to them and was warmly greeted. We walked for about a block talking of our day and what the night had in store for us. Then, when it was time to part, we exchanged hugs and Akeem peacefully said, "I love you, buddy."

At that moment I knew that the relationships I formed here are real. There was no longer any question of whether or not my presence mattered on an emotional level or whether or not I would just be forgotten in six months. This love expressed verbally between Akeem and I is something that took a long time to form and will never be easily forgotten.

TEACH P.E.?!

This year, I became a Physical Education Teacher. Can I tell you how weird this is? Very. I used to be the girl who stood in the outfield during softball, watching the ball land right next to me and expecting someone else to come get it. So this new development is slightly hilarious.

The first week or two required some creativity. The younger kids are easy to entertain. One day, I declared we were having food day and we pretended that we were spaghetti. What does that look like? First, you stand straight and very still. Then I drop you into boiling water and you become loose and dance around until everyone winds up in a pile on the middle of the plate. The kids started to ask me where the meatballs were, so after a couple plates of spaghetti, we added in some meatballs.

The older kids aren't quite as easy to entertain but, after a couple of weeks, I began having a lot of fun with them. We played kickball one day and it was probably the best game of kickball I've ever played in my life (yeah, I haven't played too many good games of kickball). They followed the rules and listened to me and learned some stuff and had fun. Pretty darn incredible. Let this be an affirmation that God can certainly work in our weakness.

WHAT DO I BRING?

THIS IS WHAT I HAVE.

STRENGTH

We live in a society that rewards strength: economic strength, physical strength, emotional strength and even spiritual strength. Over the years, I've come to realize that strength is relative.

We look strong to each other depending on the circumstance. Some are strong academically or strong on the football field. Others are strong in music or art. Strengths are needed in society, no doubt, but they can also give us a false sense of self if we're not careful. To a scientist, even a mediocre pianist may look strong. In a room full of accomplished musicians, that same pianist looks like a beginner.

All this focus on strength, however, is in complete contradiction to what we really are. We are never strong when it comes to God. There is no time or situation or circumstance that we even come close to looking strong to God. To the Creator, we are still the created. And our strength comes when we recognize our weaknesses and let Him lead the way.

God does not reward strength, He rewards faith. The ability to believe when we can't see the end. Trusting that He will protect and guide as we walk towards an unknown destination.

I admire Jesus for many reasons. He spent time with outcasts, empowered women and offered grace in situations where He was obviously right. His life and teaching make Him stand out in history and in the hearts of His followers as a remarkable leader. Jesus' kindness, courage and insight are admired not just by Christians but by Muslims, Hindus and even atheists. As a Christian, I love Jesus because He died for me. My biggest struggle is being a follower of Jesus.

When He gave an invitation to follow Him, it was with the understanding that He would be the One calling the shots at all times and that He expected a denial of self. He asks for total control.

"If anyone is to come after me let him or her deny self, take up a cross and follow."

We will struggle on this journey towards an unknown end. This not knowing the future is what makes following Jesus seem unreasonable and incredibly stupid at times, which is why I think so many struggle. The struggle is in letting go. Giving up control in a society that pushes the idea of control to the extreme. A society that rewards strength rather than weakness and leaders rather than followers. The fact is that we are not in control of anything no matter what we are told and sold. It makes complete sense to put our trust in the One who does have control and knows the end. We should embrace the fact that we are not in control and are weak. Only then will we connect to the strength of a strong and loving Creator.

A COFFEE SHOP

Coffee shops seem to be opening up in all the cool areas around my town. Think about it, one sure sign of a thriving neighborhood is a conveniently located coffee shop. It is a gathering place, a place for neighbors to come and sit with other neighbors while reading the paper or studying for an exam. Coffee shops offer not only a place to get a good latté, but also a place to relax. The comfortable sofas and free wifi provide just the right ingredients for a relaxing conversation or a quick meeting. A coffee shop is a sign of neighborhood life.

There are no coffee shops in my neighborhood. There are vacant houses, empty lots, a dollar store, a liquor store and a church or two, but no coffee shops.

Carrie is a neighbor who decided to be a good neighbor by purchasing a property in the small business square in our neighborhood. She purchased with the idea of helping to bring good business to our community. She called the afternoon after her purchase to ask if we knew anyone who would be willing to work with her to make this space a truly creative and friendly place for people to connect.

We decided to start a coffee shop. My neighborhood could use a place for neighbors to connect. A place where those who need to get away for a bit and read or study can do just that. A positive place in the neighborhood where the person fixing your latté knows who you are and what you like to drink. A safe place for the high school kids to study and for the moms to gather and talk.

This shop will employ older teens in the neighborhood. It will teach them a specific skill, but also train them in life skills: hard work, people skills, attention to detail. A coffee shop can be more than a cool place to hang out; it could be a place that community grows. It can provide the soil for building healthy relationships. It can encourage

growth by fertilizing good work habits. It can offer water to newly forming friendships. I won't be surprised to walk in soon and enjoy the sight of beautiful blossoms of neighbors caring and serving one another. A coffee shop will not solve our neighborhood's problems, but it will contribute to the solution. This could be a healthy place in a neighborhood that gets way too much bad press.

Our coffee shop will be one expression of what neighbors can do together to bring hope to a neighborhood. Hopefully, we start a trend that influences others to invest in the people around them. A trend that highlights the gifts and talents of our young people. A trend that offers job training that leads to gainful employment instead of under-employment.

We pray our little shop moves you to till community soil in your neighborhood and that you too will reap the harvest.

NOT LONG ENOUGH

Sometimes I want to say: "Hey! Whoever created Mission Year — a year isn't long enough. No fair! There is too much to be done. How can I possibly end this?" The thing is, though, my mission year isn't ending in August. There isn't a finish line that I am crossing. There isn't a trophy or pat on the back waiting for me. There isn't this "secret to life" that I am supposed to understand now.

This year has been a journey. It's been a beginning. It's been a step. It's been a process. It's been life. You can't neatly compartmentalize life. You can't just finish Mission Year. It doesn't make sense in my head that way. You change, God changes you. He'll show up for you. He will make you like Jesus, whether you know it or not. It's inevitable. And that's what Mission Year is. It's the step into seeing and experiencing that for real. Seeing and experiencing how good God really is and who He has carefully created you to be in His Kingdom here on earth.

Every decision I have made since I left Mission Year has been influenced by the relationships and experiences I had in Atlanta. My understanding of Jesus and the Gospel were so dramatically expanded that nearly all my relationships from before Mission Year were disrupted because I could no longer be the kind of Christian I was before. The comfort I had previously been blindly clinging to was now repulsive and uncomfortable. Some of those disruptions have been mended by the powerful work of Christ in my life to forgive. Some are still broken, but I know that God's Shalom will come.

At the end of Mission Year our City Director, Leroy Barber, gave us a word to take with us. My word was REMEMBER. I have reflected from that day in August 2002 until now on what it means to remember Mission Year.

I remembered when I got to Cornell by studying cities, poverty, inequality, African American Culture, Latino Culture and education.

I remembered by writing a thesis on the education reforms in New York City and whether they were improving achievement for minorities.

REMEMBER

I remembered by choosing to live in the dorms as a senior to have more opportunities to reach out to non-Christians.

I remembered by writing songs about my experience, by speaking about racial reconciliation to my InterVarsity chapter, by leading Bible Studies in my dorm about justice.

Today, I remember every day where I live and work. After I graduated from Cornell and most of my classmates were looking at apartments in Manhattan, I moved into the poorest neighborhood in the Bronx. With three other Christian guys, we are building a Christian community characterized by service, discipleship, accountability and reaching out to our neighbors.

I remember by being a teaching assistant in a 2nd Grade class at a charter school in the Bronx that is having amazing success serving a population of Latino immigrants who have a poverty rate of 92%.

I remember by caring for the environment, by buying my groceries at Trader Joes, riding the subway, not owning a car, composting, recycling.

I remember by telling the stories from my year every time I speak about justice to friends, Bible studies, churches or retreats.

I remember by reading every book I can get my hands on about justice, community, church, service, love, poverty, racism, shalom.

I remember every time I seek to love someone just to love them.

Mission Year changed everything and I am so grateful that it did. Because of Mission Year I wake up every day next to all kinds of injustice that breaks God's heart, and I seek His love and compassion to help me be His hands and feet to my neighbors.

YOU ARE INVITED

When we are invited to a party or celebration of any type there are usually three things that cause us to attend. The first is obligation; we feel we should because it would look bad if we did not. The second is the person throwing the party. Is this a close friend, an acquaintance, a co-worker? The third is who else is going. The answers to these questions make the difference not only to whether we attend or not, but how we feel about it. We either look forward to the celebration or we dread the date as it approaches.

Consider this your invitation. It is an invitation to join a celebration where the person organizing the events is God Almighty. The people attending are passionate followers of Jesus who have turned their lives over to Him and are committed to whatever He asks of them. They form communities that often swim against the stream of injustice, and put serving each other and their neighbors ahead of their own well-being. It is a beloved community because it places love at the center of its existence. These New Neighbors respond to violence with care, refuse to tolerate racism and work against poverty. They solve conflicts by sharing truth in love, and embrace trust instead of fear.

In my role as President of Mission Year and my life in the city of Atlanta, I have had the extraordinary opportunity to experience in a small way the joy that comes from such a community. Dr. Martin Luther King, Jr., in his famous "I Have A Dream" speech challenged a nation with these words: "It would be fatal for the nation to overlook the urgency of the moment." I feel the same today. It would be a lethal blow to the church if we miss this moment to discover and practice being a New Neighbor.

You have been invited to the community of the New Neighbor. Will you join?

YOU'VE BEEN
INVITED TO THE
COMMUNITY OF
NEW NEIGHBOR.

WILL YOU JOIN?

photo: 6offour.com

DATE DUE
